Greenhill Books

MODERN MILITARY RIFLES

GREENHILL MILITARY MANUALS

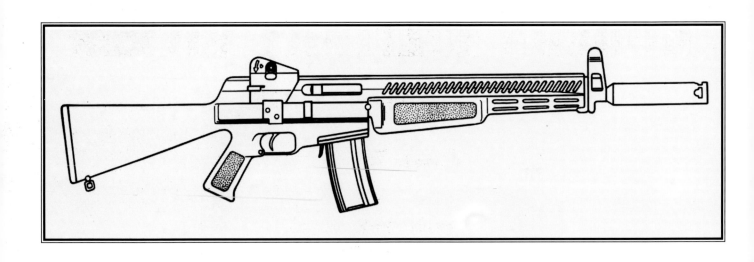

MODERN MILITARY RIFLES

GREENHILL MILITARY MANUALS

John Walter

Greenhill Books, London
Stackpole Books, Pennsylvania

For ARW and ADW

Greenhill Books

This edition of *Modern Military Rifles* first published 2001 by Greenhill Books, Lionel Leventhal Limited, Park House, 1 Russell Gardens, London NW11 9NN
www.greenhillbooks.com
and
Stackpole Books, 5067 Ritter Road, Mechanicsburg, PA 17055, USA

British Library Cataloguing in Publication Data
Walter, John, 1951–
Modern military rifles. – (Greenhill military manuals)
1. Rifles 2. Rifles – Identification
I. Title
623.4'425

ISBN 1-85367-462-1

Library of Congress Cataloging-in-Publication Data available

Designed by John Anastasio, Creative Line.
Printed and bound in Singapore by Kyodo Printing Company.

Front cover illustration: The Armalite AR-15 (M16A2) rifle, pictured here under trial, provided the basis for the Canadian 5.56mm C7.

INTRODUCTION

Inventors' thoughts turned to automatic rifles almost as soon as the Maxim machine-gun had been perfected; indeed, Maxim's first experiments had been undertaken with a Winchester lever-action rifle adapted to operate by muzzle blast, and many other patents had been filed prior to 1890. But the identity of the producer of the first truly efficient automatic weapon capable of being fired from the shoulder is still hotly contested.

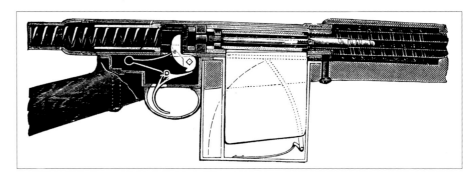

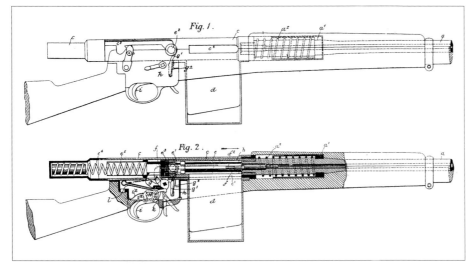

The Griffiths & Woodgate rifle, patented in 1892, was an early blowback design. The engraving is taken from the 1910 edition of Greener's The Gun and Its Development, *published long after work had ceased!*

Mannlicher's *Handmitrailleuse* has been suggested as a likely recipient of the honour, but there is no evidence that it was ever made in numbers; similarly, the Griffiths & Woodgate rifle, developed in Britain in the early 1890s, was rejected untried by the British Army and never had the significance implied by inclusion in *The Gun and Its Development* as late as 1910. It is the continual reprinting of classic works such as Greener's that so often leads us to overvalue the effect of guns that never left the prototype stage.

One of the most influential designs seems to have been the patent granted to the French Clair brothers in 1888, no matter how much English-speaking writers have decried it. Though it is highly likely that the bizarre Clair pistol never made the transition from promising idea to commercial exploitation, a few 'Clair-Éclair' gas-operated shotguns were made in Saint-Étienne in (probably) the early 1890s. Several examples still survive.

By 1900, however, many competing designs were on offer. Mannlicher had developed a variety of designs, and so, too, had Paul Mauser – or, at least, designers employed in Mauser's Oberndorf factory. However, extensive military trials almost always showed that these guns were unacceptable. They were often exceptionally clumsy and poorly balanced, but a far greater problem was posed by their stupefying complexity: analysing the strength of materials was then an infant science, and, consequently, far too many parts broke.

The Mannlicher rifles, often delayed blowbacks, were far simpler than most of those that emanated from Germany. However, virtually all military authorities were so terrified by the absence of a way of locking the breech shut at the moment of discharge (perhaps reasonable in the absence of proper metallurgical analysis) that they would not countenance the issue of guns of this type. Delayed-blowback designs were also prone to violent extraction, and the breakage of key individual components was potentially far more serious than in conventional locked-breech designs. In addition, a customary insistence that the guns should be capable of manual operation if their automatic functions failed brought additional complexity.

By 1910, designs were becoming much

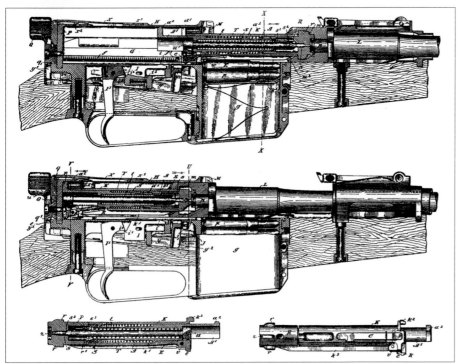

The stupefying complexity of most pre-1914 auto-loading rifles is shown by these drawings from patents granted to Mauser in 1898.

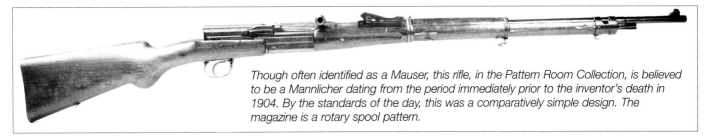

Though often identified as a Mauser, this rifle, in the Pattern Room Collection, is believed to be a Mannlicher dating from the period immediately prior to the inventor's death in 1904. By the standards of the day, this was a comparatively simple design. The magazine is a rotary spool pattern.

more serviceable. Though the British (to name one power) tried and rejected a wide range of guns, including the fiendish Tatarek, with a chain that disappeared into the butt in front of the firer's cheek, the Mondragon was being made in quantity for the Mexican Army and a variety of surprisingly efficient guns was being touted in France.

The First World War

When the First World War began in 1914, none of the experiments had been resolved. The Belgians had progressed as far as troop-trials of a promising Fabrique Nationale d'Armes de Guerre design and the French were seriously considering issuing the Meunier rifle, but most other major powers stuck doggedly to the simplicity of the bolt-action rifle.

Unfortunately, few of the auto-loading designs were successful. Among the most important problems was that posed by metallurgical science, which continued to

lag behind inventive zeal. Guns still had too many parts, too many springs, and too little strength in key components. Development work proceeded empirically, with failures being countered merely by tinkering with the design and weight distribution of individual parts.

The only rifle to have been made in quantity by this time had been the 7mm gas-operated Mondragon, locked by a rotating bolt. This gun had been designed in the early 1900s by Manuel Mondragon, a talented Mexican Army officer who had

Adopted in Mexico in 1908, made by SIG in Switzerland, but best known for its use by the German Army during the First World War, the 7x57 gas-operated Mondragon was a qualified success: it worked efficiently when clean, but jammed too easily in adverse conditions.

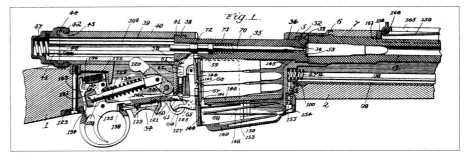

previously produced an idiosyncratic bolt-action rifle chambering a unique 'piston cartridge' and an auto-firing mechanism that presaged the 'assault at the walk' doctrine evolved in France during the First World War. Manufacture of the Mondragon, *Fusil Automatico Porfirio Diaz, Modelo de 1908* had been entrusted to Société Industrielle Suisse (SIG) of Neuhausen am Rheinfalls in Switzerland. However, very few guns had been despatched when the 1911 revolution swept Porfirio Diaz from power. The contract defaulted and the remaining guns, said to have numbered about 3000, were sold to the Germans in 1915. The Mondragon soon proved to be a better weapon that the clumsy Mauser *Fliegerselbstladekarabiner,* the last of a series of recoil-operated designs originating in 1898, but jammed far too easily in the mud of the trenches and was rapidly relegated to less important tasks.

The British experimented throughout the war with the Farquhar-Hill rifle, without ever perfecting the basic design, and it is hard to conclude that the authorities never saw Major Farquhar as anything other than a nuisance. The French, however, managed to get small quantities of the 7mm Meunier or A6 rifle into service in 1917. Though chambered for a unique cartridge, complicating logistics, these guns served until the much delayed issue of the first 8x51 RSC or *Modèle* 1917. The gas-operated RSC was long and cumbersome, weighing more than 10lb, and handicapped by its clip-loaded magazine. However, the gas-operated breech mechanism, locked by a rotating multi-lug bolt head, was surprisingly efficient and performance rose above the handicap implicit in the oddly shaped French service cartridge. Guns of this type had reached the French Army in considerable numbers prior to November 1918, along with a very few of the handier Mle 1918.

The greatest success of the First World War was unquestionably the Browning Automatic Rifle, though post-war development effectively converted it into a light machine-gun when a more enlightened approach would have concentrated on reducing its weight. At 16lb, the Browning was suitable only for the strongest men in a platoon, and issues were restricted accordingly. Yet there can be no doubt that it increased the firepower of the US infantry appreciably. More than 50,000 had been made when the war ended, though only about a quarter of these guns had been issued.

The only other belligerent to make progress with automatic-rifle design was Russia, where the *Avtomat* – developed by Vladimir Fedorov in collaboration with Vasiliy Degtyarev – had made its combat debut in 1916. A lack of production facilities kept supplies of *Avtomaty* to a minimum, and, although revived in the early 1920s, the project was never an unqualified success. Fedorov and his team deserve credit, however, for recognising the merits of comparatively low-power cartridges. The rifles made prior to 1913 had accepted the Russian 7.62x54 service-rifle cartridge, cumbersome and badly shaped though it was, but the post-1914 versions chambered the Japanese 6.5x50 semi-rimmed cartridge. Not only did this improve reliability, but the lower recoil impulse of the Japanese ammunition enhanced controllability when firing automatically.

The inter-war years

After the First World War had ended, interest in semi-automatic rifles waned virtually everywhere but in the USA and the Soviet Union. The first Soviet efforts centred on revisions of the pre-Revolutionary Fedorov *Avtomat*, whereas the USA saw the emergence of John Garand. Garand's first efforts were primer actuated, relying on the backward movement of a deep-seated primer to unlock the breech on firing, but the need for special ammunition reduced military interest appreciably. Primer-actuated Garands were tested extensively against

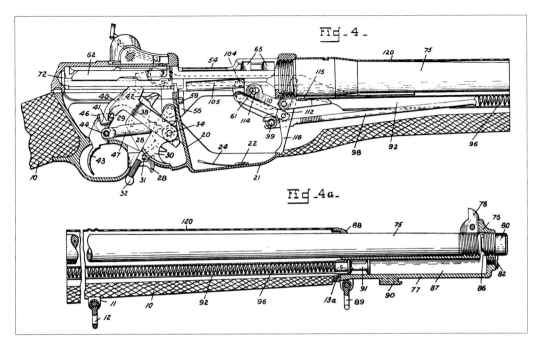

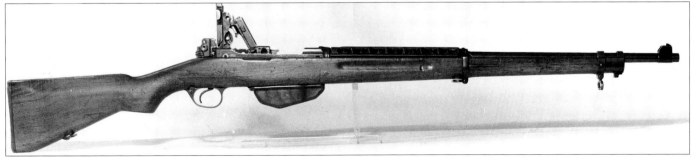

These drawings show (left) John Garand's first gas-operated .276 rifle; from a US Patent granted in 1922.

The Pedersen rifle (below) was Garand's most efficient rival, but this photograph shows why the breech mechanism was apt to strike the firer's helmet during the opening stroke. A combination of delayed-blowback operation and lubricated ammunition doomed the Pedersen in military circles.

a variety of competing designs, most notably the Thompson and, from 1924 onward, the promising delayed-blowback Pedersen, but were doomed to fail.

Garand was soon forced to abandon primer actuation, substituting a port to tap gas from the muzzle and adding a piston rod under the barrel to rotate the bolt. However, disapproval amongst the highest ranking officers in the US Army caused the promising .276 cartridge to be abandoned in February 1932, followed soon afterwards by the Pedersen rifle. This left the field to Garand, and a successful retest of the .30 T1E1 version allowed the US Army to adopt the Garand rifle as its standard infantry weapon in 1936.

Though work was undertaken in France and Germany, on desultory and small-scale bases respectively, the only other country to make real progress was the Soviet Union. A Degtyarev design had been provisionally adopted in 1931, but had been abandoned after only a few had been made. This was due largely to the parlous state of Soviet metallurgy at this date. The Degtyarev was replaced by the gas-operated Simonov, locked by a vertically moving hollow block. However, though the *Avtomaticheskaya Vintovka Simonova* (AVS or M1936) was made in substantial quantities, combat during the Winter War with Finland soon showed that

Taken during the Second World War, this Soviet official photograph shows 82mm mortar crews allegedly advancing towards German lines, but more probably on manoeuvres. The NCO in charge of the nearest mortar has an SVT 40 (Tokarev) rifle slung over his shoulder.

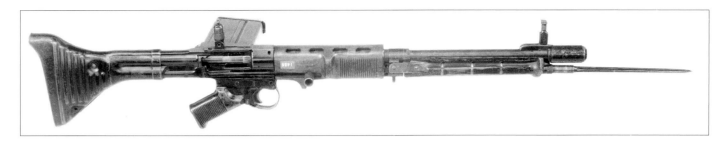

it was much too lightly built to survive arduous service.

The Simonov soon gave way to the semi-automatic Tokarev, the SVT or SVT-38. Locked by displacing the tail of the bolt downward, the Tokarev was potentially efficient – little different, indeed, from the highly successful FN FAL – but was compromised by the poor shape of the rimmed 7.62x54R rifle cartridge. The 1938-pattern rifle soon gave way to the improved 1940 pattern, with a stronger stock, and true mass production was undertaken.

Unfortunately, a combination of poor manufacturing standards and the German invasion of the Soviet Union in the summer of 1941 ultimately defeated the Tokarev. Though more than 2 million guns were made, the SVT was abandoned in favour of bolt-action Mosin-Nagants. Soviet designers continued to work on rifles chambering the 7.62x54R cartridge, but only Sergey Simonov made progress.

The German FG 42, chambered for the 7.9x57 rifle cartridge, was too revolutionary to succeed at a time during the Second World War when German metallurgy was fast declining. This first-pattern gun shows how the pistol grip was angled to enable the user to keep control when firing bursts.

By 1943, thoughts were turning to intermediate or 'assault' rifles.

The Second World War

Experimentation underway in Germany in 1918 was stopped by the Treaty of Versailles, though many technicians were ultimately able to continue work secretly in Denmark, Switzerland and even the Soviet Union. In 1933, once most of the restrictions of the hated Versailles *Diktat* had been cast away, Rheinisch-Westfälische Sprengstoff AG and Gustav Genschow & Co. AG revealed experimental cartridges adapted from the 8.15x46.5R sporting round.

None of the prototypes were successful enough to impress the *Heereswaffenamt*, the German Army weapons office, and so

Polte-Werke of Magdeburg was recruited to the programme in 1939. A 7.9mm *Kurz-Patrone* (7.9x33) had been perfected by the end of the year and, as Haenel had been given a contract for a selective-fire Maschinenkarabiner as early as April 1938, an acceptable combination of gun and cartridge appeared for the first time.

The basic Haenel rifle, usually credited to Hugo Schmeisser, was complete by 1940. However, transforming the prototype into mass-production reality was so far outside the experience of a traditional-style gunmaker that the production-engineering task was entrusted to Merz-Werke GmbH of Frankfurt am Main, a manufacturer with unrivalled experience of metal stamping, precision casting and spot-welding.

The gas tube lay above the barrel, extending forward almost to the muzzle, and the rifle fired from an open breech. Work was disrupted when, in 1942, the *Heereswaffenamt* requested the addition of a bayonet lug and a grenade launcher. The first full combat trials, undertaken in the spring of 1943 by SS Division *Wiking,* were successful enough to force Adolf Hitler to revise his poor opinion of the assault rifle concept. The Mkb 42 (H) was immediately ordered into full-scale production at the expense of the sophisticated 1942-type paratroop rifle or *Fallschirmjägergewehr* (FG 42) and the perfected semi-automatic Gew 43, derived from the Gew 41 (W). The 1941-type German rifles, one type developed by Mauser and the other by Walther, performed so badly in the Russian campaign that their owners were only too happy to discard them in favour of captured Soviet Tokarevs.

Almost concurrently with the emergence of the intermediate cartridge in Germany, the US Army embarked on an essentially similar course. The Chief of Infantry had suggested as early as 1937 that a semi-automatic rifle with an effective range of 300 yards should be developed for non-combatants. This, he argued, would be much more potent than a pistol, but light enough to be issued to men whose duties were largely away from the front line. By the beginning of May 1941, nine prototype Light Rifles had been submitted for testing, though only the Garand-designed Springfield Light Rifle – with a top-mounted box magazine and downward ejection – and George Hyde's distinctive pistol-gripped gas-operated gun (submitted by Bendix) survived the first trials.

Fortunately, a Winchester prototype reached Aberdeen Proving Ground on 9 August 1941 and performed most encouragingly. Six guns contested the trials that began on 15 September, where the modified Springfield Light Rifle (Garand), with a conventional magazine and an improved action, would have prevailed had not the perfected Winchester performed impeccably. The result was the Carbine, .30 M1 described in greater detail on page 120.

Where the Germans led, the Soviet Union elected to follow. Though experiments with small-capacity cartridges had been undertaken prior to the German invasion in the summer of 1941, no progress seems to have been made until tests had been undertaken with captured German *Maschinenkarabiner*. By the end of the year, a design team led by Semin and Elizarov had adapted the 7.9mm Kurz cartridge to produce the 7.62x39 M43 round.

Concurrently with the ammunition trials, Simonov had prepared an improved version of his 1941-type carbine for the new cartridges. The 1943-pattern carbine was smaller than its predecessor, lacked the muzzle brake and had a folding knife-blade bayonet beneath the barrel. Several hundred carbines were sent to the Byelorussian Front in 1944, where, though susceptible to dust and prone to extraction failures, they were generally well received. The untried weapon (sometimes known as the SKS-45) was promptly ordered into production, but the war ended before any series-built guns could be delivered. The opportunity was then taken to correct some of the most important flaws and the original introduction was temporarily rescinded.

The post-war period
The Mauser-Werke factory in Oberndorf fell into Allied hands after the end of the Second World War, continuing work under French supervision until the spring of 1946. Prototype assault rifles chambering .30 M1 Carbine ammunition were subsequently made in Mulhouse under the supervision of ex-Mauser engineer Ludwig Vorgrimmler.

These embodied a roller-lock system credited to Wilhelm Stähle, who had proposed it in 1942. Locked at the instant of firing, the mechanism tapped propellant gas from the bore to propel a piston backward. The piston moved the rear part of the breech block back until the locking rollers could move inward out of recesses in the receiver walls into the space created by the separation of the breech-block components. A spring in a butt tube returned the mechanism to reload the chamber and relock the breech.

By 1943, however, Mauser's technicians had discovered that the mechanism could be operated simply by allowing the backward thrust through the base of the cartridge case to unlock the rollers. Unfortunately, the military authorities were deeply suspicious of the delayed-blowback *Gerät 06.H* and had only commissioned 30 locked-breech assault rifles, the *Gerät 06* or StG 45 (M), when

the war ended.

By 1951, the focus of attention had shifted from France to Spain, whence Vorgrimmler had moved. As the Spanish Army was in desperate need of modern weapons, the Instituto Nacional de Industrias formed the Centro de Estudios Técnicos de Materiales Especiales (CETME) in Madrid to exploit the delayed-blowback roller lock. Prototype assault rifles completed in 1952 chambered a low-impulse 7.9x40 cartridge that allowed the firer to control a gun weighing less than 4kg when working automatically.

Early in 1954, impressed by the CETME rifles but uncertain of the manufacturing technology, the Spanish government invited Heckler & Koch to resolve mass-

production problems. Promising trials of these pre-production 'straight line' 7.9mm guns – consisting largely of sheet-steel pressings, with the cocking handle in a tube above the barrel – were undertaken in Germany in 1955, where the rifle was then revised for the US .30 T65 cartridge. The ultimate result was the Heckler & Koch G3.

The other major European success came in the form of the SAFN rifle, based on pre-war Belgian prototypes and a few Rifles, 7.92mm, Self-Loading, Experimental Model No. 1 (SLEM No. 1) made at Enfield in 1944 to a design prepared by Dieudonné Saive and emigré FN technicians attached to the Small Arms Group, Cheshunt. Though sufficient

Among the greatest successes of the post-war era has been the Kalashnikov, seen here in Yugoslav-made form.

rifles to undertake field trials were ordered in 1946, few were made until Fabrique Nationale recommenced production in Herstal in 1949. The SAFN rifle was made in substantial numbers, but succeeded only in laying the basis for the extraordinarily successful FN FAL.

Whereas most Western powers were content – in some cases, insistent – on retaining full-power infantry rifle cartridges, designers in the Soviet Union were keener to perpetuate the German-style assault rifle. The first trial of an *Avtomat,* a hybrid of rifle and submachine-gun, was undertaken with a Sudaev design that soon proved to be too clumsy. Then came the Kalashnikov, readied in a factory in Alma-Ata in 1946 with assistance from a designers' collective.

A handful of *Avtomaty sistemy Kalashnikova, optniy obr. 1946g* (trials pattern, 1946) showed such great promise that a process of refinement began in the Tula ordnance factory. The 1947 No. 1 prototype differed considerably from the 1946 pattern, gaining the familiar closed-top breech cover with an ejection port on the right side. It passed field testing with flying colours and was adopted for service in 1949. It has since been made in many guises – AK, AKM, AK-74 – but they are all mechanically similar to the original trials guns of 1947.

The gradual envelopment of the central European states into the Soviet bloc affected Czechoslovakia, which had only recently emerged from German occupation. Prior to the 'nationalisation' of 1948, the Czechoslovakians had impressed substantial quantities of old German semi-automatic rifles into service, but the army wanted a new weapon based on an intermediate cartridge. A 7.5x45 round was successfully tested in 1947, and prototype rifles were submitted by Česká Zbrojovka of Strakonice – one operated by gas, another a blowback – to compete against the gas-operated weapons championed by Československá Zbrojovka of Brno.

The ČZ 147, designed by Josef Kratochvil, was deemed the most promising prototype; the army was willing to adopt the perfected 7.5mm ČZ 475, but pressure brought to bear by the USSR to standardise calibres led to the belated appearance of the 7.62mm ČZ 493. Comparative trials resolved in favour of the ZK 472, but a decision was taken in March 1950 to standardise an improved ČZ 493 with a laterally swinging knife bayonet on the right side of the fore-end. This became the ČZ 502, and finally the vz. 52 service rifle. Intriguingly, the Czechoslovakian authorities reverted to the 7.5mm

cartridge, against the will of the Soviet Union, apparently because production facilities were already in existence. This independence ended in 1957, when the vz. 52 was belatedly (and not particularly successfully) adapted for the 7.62x39 M43 round.

In Belgium, meanwhile, work had continued to improve the SAFN. A prototype assault rifle chambering the German 7.9x33 cartridge had been demonstrated in 1948 at the Fabrique Nationale proving ground in Zutendael, and, by 1950, work was centring on standard (No. 1) and 'bullpup' (No. 2) rifles. The latter was soon abandoned, owing to poor handling characteristics and worries that the firer's head was threatened if a cartridge-case head failed. The No. 1 rifle, however, was enlarged in 1951 to chamber the semi-experimental British .280 (7x49) and the rejection of this cartridge by the US Army eventually persuaded FN to rechamber the assault rifle for the experimental American .30 T65.

The perfected *Fusil Automatique Léger* (FAL) was a runaway success after a slow start. Beginning with an export order for Venezuela in 1953, for guns chambering the British .280 cartridge, FALs have been sold to the armed forces of more than 60 countries. Production has been licensed throughout the world, typical of this group being the Brazilian M1964, the British L1A1 and the Canadian C1, described in the Directory.

Though the FAL satisfied many European NATO-aligned armies, the French declined to comply with the standardisation programme and instead embarked on the development of a weapon of their own. Prototype locked-breech assault rifles replaced unsuccessful delayed-blowback patterns, embodying the gas system and Tokarev-type tilting-block lock of the MAS 49/56, but with direct impingement of gas on the face of the bolt carrier substituted by a short-stroke piston. The perfected *Fusil d'Assaut MAS 62*, made in small numbers in Saint-Étienne, was tentatively adopted in 1967, but the trend towards small calibres led to a reassessment of requirements and work began instead on a 5.56mm design (FA MAS, q.v.).

While the Belgians were developing the FAL, and the CETME rifle was being perfected in Spain, the ArmaLite Division of Fairchild Engine & Airplane Corporation had been formed to promote guns embodying aluminium alloy parts and foam-filled synthetic furniture. The mechanism of the AR-3, designed by ArmaLite's chief engineer Eugene Stoner, was a variation of the rotating bolt patented in the 1930s by Melvin Johnson combined with a pistonless direct-impingement gas system. The AR-3 led to the AR-10, the third prototype being tested successfully at Fort Benning in 1955. Then came the improved AR-10B, with the gas tube above the barrel, an improved bolt carrier, and a rifled steel liner inside an alloy barrel casing. Trials revealed that the ArmaLite was in need of further development, and ended spectacularly, early in 1957, when a bullet came out of the side of the barrel.

ArmaLite had granted manufacturing rights to the state-owned Artillerie-Inrichtingen in 1959, hoping that a Dutch government order would follow. The perfected AR-10 finished a creditable second to the FAL in the South African trials of 1960, but failure during an endurance test lost an order from the Nicaraguan national guard and – when the Dutch adopted the FAL – Artillerie-Inrichtingen lost interest. Work on the 7.62mm rifle ceased, but attempts to develop a small-calibre derivative were destined to be far more successful.

The small-calibre revolution

Tests undertaken in the USA in 1952–3, with an M2 Carbine rechambered for a shortened .222 Remington cartridge, demonstrated the value of small-calibre high-velocity bullets and light automatic rifles. Though experiments incurred official disapproval, the US Army authorities prepared a specification in 1957 for a small-calibre selective-fire rifle with a magazine capacity of at least 20 rounds but a laden weight no greater than 6lb.

ArmaLite engineers Robert Fremont and James Sullivan subsequently altered an AR-10 to fire a modified .222 Remington round, producing a weapon that weighed 6.12lb with a loaded 25-round magazine and was merely 37.5in long. About 20 AR-15 guns were then made for trials, the most obvious characteristics among the markings being the encircled Pegasus trademark on the left side of the magazine housing and the use of 'Patents pending'.

Differences of opinion amongst army experts had, meanwhile, increased the performance requirements from 300yd to 500yd – solved by ArmaLite by substituting the .223 Remington cartridge (known prior to 1959 as the .222 Remington Special) – but the AR-15 then gained a rival in the form of the .224 Winchester Light-Weight Military Rifle (WLAR), created largely by amalgamating the best features of the company's previous auto-loaders.

Tests undertaken in 1958 with the AR-15, at Fort Benning, Aberdeen Proving Ground and Fort Greely, were all highly

A CAR-15 fitted with a 40mm M203 grenade launcher and a 100-round MWG drum magazine.

successful. Doubts about the lethality of small-diameter bullets persisted, but the AR-15 and the WLAR had performed better than the 7.62mm T44E4. The AR-15 charging handle was moved to the rear of the receiver, the safety position on the selector was altered to point forward, barrel weight was increased, and a flash suppressor was added. Magazine capacity was reduced to 20 rounds in compensation for weight that had been added elsewhere.

Unfortunately, the small-calibre high-velocity concept was encountering such fierce opposition from the Office of the Chief of Ordnance that .222 was summarily rejected in favour of an 'optimal' .258. Trials recommenced at the beginning of December 1958, but then came a bombshell: the Chief of Ordnance directed that the 7.62mm M14 (as the T44E4 had become) was the only rifle suitable for military use. Fairchild lost interest in the AR-15 and had soon sold the licence to Colt.

Small-scale sales to Malaysia and India had already been made by the time Colt completed its first rifles at the end of 1959, and claims were soon being made that the AR-15 could fire far more shots without cleaning than any rival. The USAF, actively seeking to replace obsolescent M2 Carbines, then reviewed the AR-15. Experiments confirmed that the guns were accurate and reliable, and the rifle was grudgingly cleared for USAF scrutiny. The air force trials were so encouraging that a request was made to Congress for 8500 guns. The approach was initially rejected, but affairs in Vietnam could not be ignored; in January 1962, therefore, the 5.56mm Rifle AR-15 (later XM16, then M16) was classified as USAF standard. Congress had soon approved an order for 20,000 rifles for the USAF, Navy SEALs and American advisers in Vietnam. Where the air force led, the army was soon forced to follow by the failure of the SPIW project, acquiring more than 300 XM-16 rifles for trials against the M14 and the Kalashnikov. And, after overruling many objectors, the Secretary of the Army recommended the purchase of up to 100,000 AR-15 rifles for army airborne units and special forces.

Major faults were blamed, with justification, on poor quality control of guns and ammunition. Minor problems continued to arise with exasperating frequency; however, as the Secretary of Defense had ordered that only unavoidable changes should be made, much correctional work was left undone.

Rifling making one complete turn in 12 inches was accepted in July 1963 to safeguard bullet performance in sub-zero conditions, and an auxiliary bolt-closing mechanism in the form of a plunger designed by Foster Sturtevant was added to the rear right side of the XM-16 receiver above the pistol grip. This created the XM16E1. The XM16E1 was eventually standardised as the M16A1, which served the US Army throughout the embroilment in Vietnam. Details will be found in the relevant section of the directory, or in Edward C. Ezell's magisterial work, The *Black Rifle. M16 Retrospective* (Collector Grade Publications, Inc., 1987).

Interest in the assault rifle has taken disparate paths. Many lesser armies have been content to buy guns from a handful of established manufacturers: Colt, Fabrique Nationale, Heckler & Koch and Beretta among them. Some have developed guns of their own, either on the basis of well-proven designs (customarily the Kalashnikov) and occasionally on the basis of new ideas.

Typical of the Kalashnikov path are the Israeli Galil, which owes its detail to the Finnish m/62, and a selection of guns that has emanated from Kraguyevac in what was once Yugoslavia. The Finnish guns were originally made in two patterns: Type A provided by Sako, with a vertical post between the trigger lever and the magazine and a fluted fore-end pierced with ventilation holes, and the Valmet-made Type B with a conventional trigger guard released by a spring catch on the back of the pistol grip. The Valmet design was accepted as the fm/60, delivered for field trials in the winter of 1960, and soon progressed to the m/62 (pages 56–57).

In Britain, the story was very different – yet in some ways typical of a country in which the most successful weapons have often been designed by foreigners. Trials to find a new small-calibre service rifle for the British Army began in the late 1960s, though the promising 6.25x43 cartridge tested in 1969–71 soon gave way to a 4.85x49 development (1973). Work then began on a suitable rifle, the project team being led by the late John Weeks, co-author of *Military Small Arms of the Twentieth Century* (Krause Publications, seventh edition, 2000) but then a British Army officer. The history of the rifle is covered in greater detail in the Directory (pages 41-42), but it is fair to say that success has eluded it. Horror stories of poor design and bad manufacture abound, and it cannot be long before the rifle (like the Light Support Weapon before it) is replaced by something more efficient. It may not be entirely coincidental that the worst problems seem to date from the change during the development phase from the 4.85mm cartridge to the ubiquitous 5.56x45.

Beyond the rifle

Assault rifles, often with origins that date back 50 years or more, still equip the world's armed forces. Specialised equipment may be issued for sniping and special duties, and interesting

FN Herstal has staked much on the development of its 5.7mm P-90 Personal Defence Weapon, specifically designed for non-combatants.

low-power weapons such as the FN Herstal 5.7mm P-90 Personal Defence Weapon may be suited to non-combatant personnel, but the ArmaLite and the Kalashnikov will soldier on for many years.

Attempts have often been made to perfect weapons that are technically superior to existing rifles, easier to make and simpler to use. The most obvious experimentation has concerned ammunition; in particular, the development of an entirely self-contained cartridge that can consume all of itself excepting the bullet on firing. This, of course, as there is no need for extractors and ejecting systems, simplifies the breech. Heckler & Koch has come nearest to success, the 4.7mm G11 rifle falling victim, on the verge of success, to the costly reunification of Germany. Though the project was put on hold, the acceptance of the conventional rotating-bolt

5.56x45 G36 probably spells the end of a fascinating development history.

Alternative approaches have been taken in the USA, where a succession of acronyms has camouflaged some exceptionally interesting guns. The Special Purpose Infantry Weapon (SPIW) programme was a costly failure, as attempts to marry flechette ammunition with grenade launchers was always likely to provide problems; few of the combination weapons made since the Middle Ages have been anything other than limited successes, as the gains in one area are customarily balanced by losses in another.

Participants in the Advanced Combat Rifle (ACR) programme included submissions by Steyr-Mannlicher and the AAI Corporation, both of which fired high-velocity discarding-sabot flechette ammunition; by Colt, in the form of an improved M16A2 firing duplex-ball rounds; and from Heckler & Koch, with a variant of the G11 caseless-cartridge rifle. The AAI gun was perhaps the most interesting, as it was capable, in some guises, of firing three cartridges in exceptionally rapid succession. The use of flechettes, with an ultra-flat trajectory arising from a velocity approaching 5000ft/sec, allowed sights to be reduced virtually to a top rib.

Unfortunately for the US Army, none of

The Heckler & Koch G11K3, chambering a unique 4.7mm self-consuming caseless cartridge, came close to success. Unfortunately, shortage of funding persuaded the Bundeswehr *to take the conventional G36 instead.*

the guns achieved the desired 100 per cent improvement in 'first round hit probability', and the program closed about 1990. It was replaced by the OCIW (Objective Combat Infantry Weapon) series, with a similar lack of success. Interestingly, the idea of firing at least two rounds at 2000rpm or more has recently reappeared in the Russian AN-94 (Nikonov) rifle. High-velocity flechette ammunition still intrigues many designers, and who knows which of the other ideas will reappear next…

The Directory features a selection of the guns that have achieved service status since 1950. This omits designs – such as the Soviet Tokarev or US Johnson rifles – that served during the Second World War but had no lasting effects on post-1950 affairs.

Dimensions and performance data have been taken, where possible, from official handbooks and literature produced by the manufacturers. However, as this material is not always comprehensive, information (and conversions of dimensions) has occasionally been added. These 'unofficial' alterations are indicated with an asterisk (*), though the remaining figures remain as originally written.

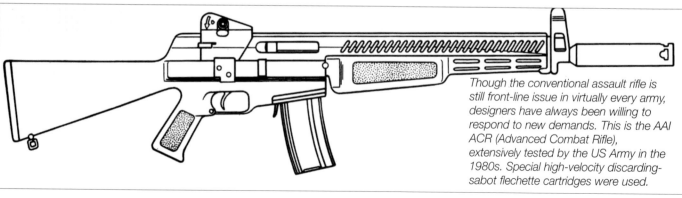

Though the conventional assault rifle is still front-line issue in virtually every army, designers have always been willing to respond to new demands. This is the AAI ACR (Advanced Combat Rifle), extensively tested by the US Army in the 1980s. Special high-velocity discarding-sabot flechette cartridges were used.

Directory

Contents

Fara 83 Argentina

The Argentine needs for semi-automatic rifles were satisfied in the early 1950s largely by Fabrique Nationale d'Armes de Guerre, suppliers of a few thousand .30-06 Mle 49 (SAFN) – apparently for the navy – and then in the early 1960s of the first 7.62mm FALs. When work ceased in 1981, more than 130,000 licence-built copies had been made by Fábrica Militar de Armas Portatiles of Rosario, Santa Fé. Many of them had been sold to Colombia, Honduras, Peru and Uruguay.

The replacement for the FAL was initially seen as the indigenous 5.56mm FARA 83, a conventional-looking gun with a glass-reinforced synthetic fibre butt that can be swung forward along the right side of the receiver and a grooved fore-end that accepts the bipod legs. The backsight has two open notches (200m, 400m) and a special tritium-insert 100m position for use in poor light.

Unfortunately, after a single production run of about 1250 FARAs in 1985, the Argentine treasury withheld funding. The completion of issue, therefore, remains in limbo; and it seems more likely that other guns (e.g., the FN FNC) will simply be purchased when required.

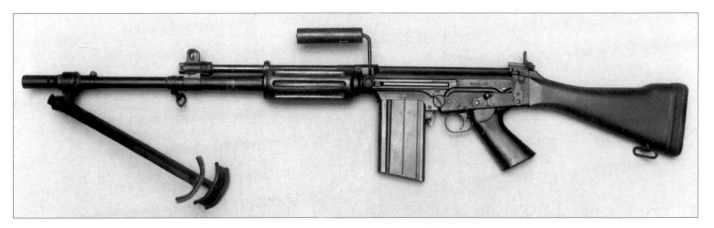

A typical Argentine 7.62mm FALO-type light support weapon, made by FAP, captured by the British during the Falklands campaign of 1982.

Assault rifle: Fusil Automatico del Republica de Argentina Modelo 83, FARA 83
Made by Fábrica Militar de Armas Portatiles Domingo Matheu, Rosario, Santa Fé

Specification Standard infantry rifle
 Data from Ian Hogg, *The Greenhill Military Small Arms Data Book* (1999)
Calibre 5.56mm (.223in)
Cartridge 5.56x45, rimless
Operation Gas operated, selective fire
Locking system Rotating bolt
Length 1000mm (39.37in) with butt extended; 745mm (29.33in) with butt folded
Weight 3.95kg (8.71lb*) with empty magazine (?)
Barrel 452mm (17.8in), 6 grooves, right-hand twist
Magazine 30-round detachable box
Rate of fire 750rds/min
Muzzle velocity 965m/sec (3166ft/sec) with SS109 ball ammunition

The 5.56mm FARA 83 seems unlikely ever to equip the Argentine armed forces.

This futuristic 'bullpup', tapping gas from the barrel to strike a bolt-carrier guide rod and rotate the bolt, was developed specifically for the Austrian Army. The first guns were delivered in 1978. By 1980, the standard selective-fire rifles had been christened AUG-A1 to distinguish them from the AUG-P (*Polizei* or Police), a short-barrelled selective-fire or semi-automatic version, firing from a closed bolt.

Austrian-made rifles have been used by many military and paramilitary organisations, among large-scale purchasers being Australia, Ecuador, Eire, Oman, Saudi Arabia and Tunisia. The Lithgow small-arms factory in Australia now makes the AUG under licence as the 5.56mm Rifle F8.

The AUG is created from six modules: barrel, receiver (cast integrally with the optical-sight bracket), trigger, bolt, magazine and butt. This allows it to be configured as a light support weapon, a carbine or a submachine-gun, and ejection can be changed from right to left merely by exchanging the bolt and ejection-port cover.

A black or olive green synthetic frame is common to all sub-variants, though barrels can vary from 350mm to a 621mm heavyweight pattern with a bipod attached. The receiver is usually found with an integral optical sight, but an open backsight or ('N' pattern only) a conventional optical-sight mount may be substituted.

Differing triggers and bolts allow guns to operate semi- or fully automatically, or from open or closed bolt position; light pressure on the trigger fires single shots and, where appropriate, strong pressure allows the mechanism to cycle automatically. Prong-type flash suppressors are standard, a pivoting hand grip lies in front of the trigger guard, a safety bolt runs laterally through the frame, and distinctive transparent plastic magazines show how many cartridges remain.

The 5.56mm AUG dismantled into its principal components.

An AUG with a Simrad electro-optical sight in addition to the standard 1.5x telescopic sight built into the carrying handle.

Assault rifle: Armee-Universal-Gewehr (AUG), also known as the Sturmgewehr 77 or StG. 77
Made by Steyr-Daimler-Puch AG, Steyr (to 1990), and Steyr-Mannlicher GmbH (1990 onwards)

Specification Standard infantry pattern
Data taken from manufacturer's manual, *Army Universal Assault Rifle 'Steyr'...,* undated (*c.* 1980)
Calibre 5.56x45mm (.223in)
Operation Gas operated, selective fire
Locking system Rotating bolt
Length 790mm (31in)
Weight 3.6kg (7.9lb) without magazine
Barrel 508mm (20in), 6 grooves, right-hand twist
Magazine 30- or 42-round detachable box
Rate of fire 680–850rds/min
Muzzle velocity 970m/sec (3182ft/sec) with standard ball ammunition

A Steyr-made AUG equipped to launch a rifle grenade.

Adopted by the Austrian Army in 1969, and then by military and police forces throughout the world, this embodies a heavy version of the standard Steyr-Mannlicher sporting rifle action with the receiver extending forward to enclose the chamber. A spool magazine was originally standardised, but has now been joined by an optional ten-round detachable box. Most of the metal parts of military-issue SSGs are phosphated to eliminate reflections.

The original SSG 69 had a walnut or Cycolac stock, the latter being brown or olive green; spacers could be fitted to adjust the length of the butt. Most military-issue rifles will be found with optical sights, though otherwise similar Match Target guns have been offered with competition-type aperture sights.

The standard rifle was redesignated P-I when the P-II appeared; a .243 Winchester chambering option being introduced at the same time.

P-II Introduced in 1988, this has a heavy barrel and an enlarged bolt-handle knob.

P-III A 1992-vintage variant offering aperture-sight bases, a heavy 600mm

The breech of the SSG 69, showing the original spatulate bolt handle.

barrel, and an American-made synthetic H-S Precision stock.

P-IV Chambered only for the .308 Winchester round, this has a Cycolac stock and a barrel measuring merely 425mm without its flash-hider. It was introduced with the P-III in 1992.

Sniper rifle: Schafschützengewehr 69 or SSG 69
Made by Steyr-Mannlicher GmbH, Steyr

Specification Standard version
   Data from John Walter, *Rifles of the World* (Krause Publications, second edition, 1998)
Calibre 7.62mm (.300in)
Cartridge 7.62x51 NATO, rimless

Operation Manually operated
Locking system Rotating bolt
Length 1130mm (44.5in)
Weight 3.95kg (8.71lb), without sights
Barrel 650mm (25.6in), 4 grooves, right-hand twist
Magazine 5-round detachable spool
Rate of fire NA
Muzzle velocity 820m/sec (2690ft/sec) with standard SS77 ball ammunition

A typical P-II SSG M69, with the enlarged bolt handle and steadying tripod.

Work that had begun prior to the Second World War and continued with the abortive British SLEM rifle was completed in Herstal in 1947–8. The perfected rifle was adopted by the Belgian Army as the *Fusil Semi-automatique* Mle 1949, though it has also been known as the SAFN (Semi-Automatic, Fabrique Nationale). The term ABL, often misleadingly applied as a designation, arose from the property mark – *Armée Belge Leger* – which was a combination of French *(Armée Belge)* and Flemish *(Leger Belge).*

The Mle 49 has a tall squared receiver, carrying the backsight and prominent sight-guards, and a conventional pistol-grip wooden stock. A handguard runs from the chamber to the backsight/gas-port block, and a bayonet bar is fitted beneath the muzzle. The magazine can be loaded from chargers, appropriate guides being milled in the receiver top. Muzzle brake/compensators were optional, and guns could be supplied to order in semi-automatic or selective-fire versions.

A sniper rifle was also issued in small numbers, accompanied by a telescope sight made by Société Belge d'Optique et d'Instruments de Précision, but was replaced first by optically sighted FALs and then by FN-Mauser bolt-action rifles.

Though several large-scale export orders had been attracted by 1952, the Mle 49 rifle was soon found to be unsuitable for arduous use. It handled awkwardly, owing in no small way to the excessive height of the receiver, and failures in the trigger system could result in the action 'running away' – emptying the magazine in an instant.

The experimental British SLEM rifle (top) contrasted with the perfected SAFN (bottom). The similarities are obvious.

The Mle 49 had soon been replaced with the FAL in Belgian service. However, SAFN-type guns were supplied from Herstal to the Belgian Congo (Zaire), Colombia, Egypt, Indonesia, Luxembourg and Venezuela.

Semi-automatic rifle: Fusil Semi-automatique Mle 1949 (SAFN)
Made by Fabrique Nationale d'Armes de Guerre, Herstal-lèz-Liége

Specification Standard infantry rifle
  Data from Ian Hogg, *The Greenhill Military Small Arms Data Book* (1999)

Calibre 7.9mm (.311in)
Cartridge 7.62x51 NATO, rimless (also offered in 7x57, 7.65x53 or .30-06)
Operation Gas operated, semi-automatic fire only
Locking system Tilting bolt
Length 1116mm (44.0in)
Weight 4.31kg (9.5lb*)
Barrel 590mm (22.25in), 6 grooves, right-hand twist
Magazine 10-round integral box
Rate of fire NA
Muzzle velocity 730m/sec (2400ft/sec)

FN FAL

Belgium

The perfected FAL was adopted by the Belgian Army in 1956. It originally had charger guides on the receiver; a smooth muzzle with neither grenade launcher nor flash suppressor; a nose-cap wooden butt; and a plain butt plate without a trap. A tubular bayonet doubled as a flash suppressor/ compensator if necessary, and the handguard was usually injection-moulded plastic. A synthetic butt and fore-end were standardised in 1963. The fore-end may be grooved to accept the legs of the bipod, even though this is rarely present on infantry rifles. Three

cooling slots are standard.

Belgian FAL-type guns have been supplied to many military forces, ranging from Bahrain to Zaire, and guns have been made under licence in many countries (e.g., Britain, Brazil, Argentina). Details of these may be found from the three-volume set published by Collector Grade Publications or, in the form of a brief listing, in John Walter, *Rifles of the World* (second edition, 1998).

Type 50-00 This designation was applied from the 1970s onward to distinguish the standard or infantry-

pattern selective-fire FAL, with nylon furniture, a fixed butt and a tubular flash suppressor. Finish is usually durable grey phosphating.

Type 50-64 Para This is similar mechanically to the standard infantry rifle, excepting that the addition of a folding tube-frame butt requires the breech-block return spring to be

Three typical FAL rifles: a standard 7.62mm FN FAL Type 50-00, with synthetic furniture (below); a heavy-barrel FALO Type 50-41 (above right); and an MD-1 produced under licence in Brazil.

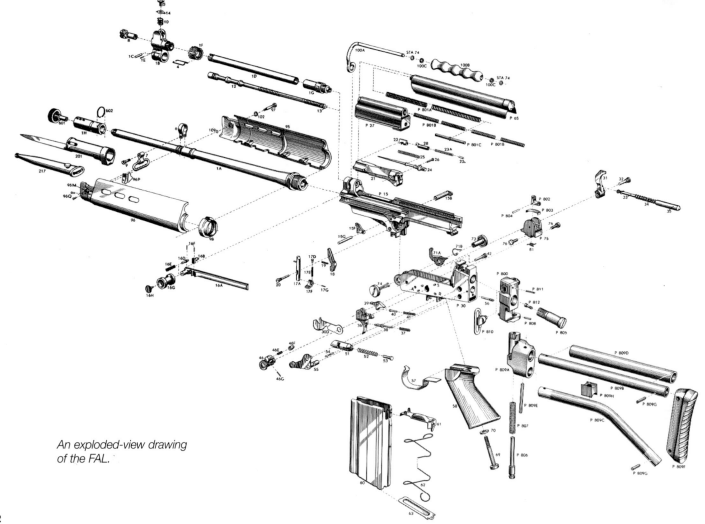

An exploded-view drawing of the FAL.

The FAL, shown here in its 'Type Para' folding-butt form, has been proven in combat throughout the world.

Auto-loading rifle: Fusil Automatique Leger (FAL) or Light Automatic Rifle (LAR)
Made by Fabrique Nationale d'Armes de Guerre, Herstal-lèz-Liége

Specification Standard Type 50-00 infantry rifle
Data from manufacturer's handbook, *Light Automatic Rifle L.A.R. Cal. 7.62mm NATO...Operator's Manual*, dated February 1983
Calibre 7.62mm (.300in)
Cartridge 7.62x51 NATO, rimless
Operation Gas operated, selective fire
Locking system Titling bolt
Length 1100mm (43.31in*)
Weight 4.325kg (9.53lb*) without magazine; a full 20-round magazine added 730g (1.61lb*)
Barrel 533mm (20.98in*), 4 grooves, right-hand twist
Magazine 20-round detachable box
Rate of fire 650–700rds/min
Muzzle velocity 840m/sec (2756ft/sec*) with SS77 ball ammunition

contained entirely within the receiver. The cocking handle can be folded down against the receiver to prevent snagging.

Type 50-63 Para Only 1020mm (40.15in) long, or about 770 (30.3in) with the butt folded, this shortened gun had a folding cocking handle and a 300m battle sight. The hold-open and carrying handle of the longer 50-64 Para were omitted. Empty weight was about 3.75kg (8.27lb).

Type 50-41 (Fusil Automatique Lourd, LAR HB) Dating from 1958, this heavy-barrel FAL has a sturdier handguard, a combination flash suppressor/muzzle brake, and a folding bipod. However, the FALO was never successful in the intended light support role. This is partly due to the fixed barrel, which rapidly overheated if fire was sustained, but also to an unexplained tendency to fire twice and then jam on the third round of automatic fire. Many champions of the FAL never bought heavy-barrel guns, and purchasers such as Australia rapidly withdrew them from front-line service to serve snipers. A FALO is typically 1150mm (45.28in) long, weighs about 6kg (13.23lb) without its 30-round magazine, and has a sliding 600m aperture sight.

FN CAL

Belgium

The first attempts were made to adapt the FAL to 5.56mm (.223) in 1963, but the tilting-block locking system lacked sufficient camming action to ease spent cases out of the chamber. Trials showed that extraction was not reliable enough and the first prototypes of the *Carabine Automatique Légère* were not demonstrated until 1967. Series production began in 1969.

The gun retains the proven gas system and trigger of the FAL, but a conventional rotating bolt has replaced the tilting block. The selector lies directly above the trigger on the left side of the receiver, markings 'S', '1', '3' and 'A' signifying safety, single shots, bursts, and fully automatic operation respectively. The guns may be accompanied by a distinctive tubular flash-hider bayonet.

The CAL resembles its 7.62mm predecessor externally, and can be found with either a fixed synthetic butt or a folding tubular pattern. The fore-end is a complex sheet-steel pressing with ventilation slots. By 1975, however, the rifle had been abandoned.

Too expensive and still afflicted by extraction failures, it had appeared at a time when many military authorities still doubted the efficiency of 5.56mm ammunition. Gabon and Lebanon each purchased a few thousand rifles, but the CAL was replaced by the sturdier and much more successful FNC.

Auto-loading rifle: Carabine Automatique Légère, CAL
Made by Fabrique Nationale d'Armes de Guerre, Herstal-lèz-Liége, *c.* 1966–74

Specification Standard fixed-butt pattern
Data from Ian Hogg, *The Greenhill Military Small Arms Data Book* (1999)
Calibre 5.56mm (.223in)
Operation Gas operated, selective fire
Locking system Rotating bolt
Length 978mm (38.5in)
Weight 2.94kg (6.5lb*)
Barrel 469mm (18.46in), 6 grooves, right-hand twist
Magazine 20-, later 30-round detachable box
Rate of fire 850rds/min
Muzzle velocity 975m/sec (3200ft/sec) with M193 ball ammunition

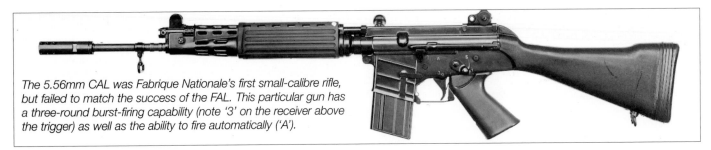

The 5.56mm CAL was Fabrique Nationale's first small-calibre rifle, but failed to match the success of the FAL. This particular gun has a three-round burst-firing capability (note '3' on the receiver above the trigger) as well as the ability to fire automatically ('A').

FN FNC   Belgium

The successor to the CAL described previously, the FNC was developed hurriedly in 1975–7 to participate in NATO standardisation trials. However, the rifle was withdrawn from competition as soon as it was realised that the submission had been made too early in the developmental process. By 1980, the basic gas and rotating-bolt locking systems were performing efficiently enough and concern centred on simplified production techniques. The FNC was successfully entered in trials in Sweden in 1981–2, eventually becoming

the Ak-5 (q.v.) and finally, after issuing FNCs to airborne forces for some years, the Belgian government indicated that the 5.56mm gun would gradually replace the 7.62mm FAL in universal service after 1989.

The FNC is also currently being made under licence in Indonesia, the ultimate result of an order placed in 1982 by the Indonesian air force. The government signed a licensing agreement in 1984, and assembly is believed to have begun in the state arsenal in 1987. These guns display a Garuda mark on the receiver or

magazine housing. The FNC has also been sold in quantity throughout Africa, the Middle East, South and Central America.

Model 90.00 These guns have a folding skeleton butt of tubular steel, but a fixed polyamide butt can be obtained on request; the bayonet, where used, is a variant of the US M7. The barrels and chambers are chromed to minimise the effects of propellant fouling, and a three-round burst-fire mechanism can be fitted whenever required. No distinction was originally drawn between the two differing

The 5.56mm FN FNC, the replacement for the CAL, has been adopted by Belgium and Sweden. This optically-sighted example dates from 1983.

Type 7000 Mechanically identical with the Type 6000, this had rifling suited to the M193 bullet.

Auto-loading rifle: Fabrique Nationale Carabine, FNC
Made by FN Herstal SA, Herstal-lèz-Liége, 1982 to date

Specification Standard infantry rifle
 Data from manufacturer's handbook, *FN Carbine F.N.C. Calibre 5,56x45mm. Operator's Manual,* dated March 1982
Calibre 5.56mm (.223in)
Operation Gas operated, selective fire
Locking system Rotating bolt
Length 997mm (39.25in*) with butt extended; 766mm (30.16in*) with butt folded
Weight 3.8kg (8.38lb*) without magazine; a loaded 30-round magazine weighs 560g (1.23lb*)
Barrel 449mm (17.68in*) without flash suppressor, 6 grooves, right-hand twist
Magazine 30-round detachable box
Rate of fire 625–700rds/min
Muzzle velocity 915m/sec (3002ft/sec*) with SS109 ball ammunition

rifling patterns, making a turn in 12in and 7in to suit the Belgian 5.56mm SS109 and US .223 M193 bullets respectively.

Model 92.00 Introduced in 1979, the standard short-barrelled FNC could be supplied with 1-in-12 or 1-in-7 rifling. According to a leaflet produced in September 1981, *FNC 5.56x45mm NATO,* the guns are 911mm (35.87in*) long, have 363mm (14.29in*) barrels,

and weigh 3.7kg (8.16lb*).

Type 0000 The post-1980 designation for the Model 90.00 with rifling suited to the SS109 bullet, making a turn in 305mm (12in).

Type 2000 This was once the Model 90.00 adapted for the M193 bullet, rifled with a turn in 178mm (7in).

Type 6000 A short-barrelled carbine rifled for the SS109 bullet.

This is essentially a variant of the FN Mle 30 military rifle and its post-war derivative, the .30-06 Mle 1950. The magazine well of the latter was lengthened to accept the 63mm cartridge case of the .30-06 round, which was 10mm longer than the standard Belgian 7.65mm pattern. A groove was cut vertically across the chamber face, and the guides on the receiver bridge accepted the standard American charger.

Eventually, in the early 1970s, a refinement of the short rifle, embodying the same Mauser-type bolt action, was adapted for precision shooting. These guns have a heavy barrel, an adjustable trigger, and a butt that can not only be lengthened with wooden spacers but can also slide vertically.

Most rifles have STANAG-compatible mounts for optical or electro-optical sights, though a few will be seen with Anschütz aperture sights. A rail set into the underside of the fore-end accepts a hand-stop, a sling mount or even a MAG-type bipod. Some guns have flash eliminators on their muzzles, and some are fitted with optional ten-round magazines.

Bolt-action sniper rifle: Fusil Modèle 30-11
Made by FN Herstal SA, Herstal-lèz-Liége, *c.* 1975–87

Specification Standard pattern
  Data from Ian Hogg, *The Greenhill Military Small Arms Data Book* (1999)
Calibre 7.62mm (.300in)
Cartridge 7.62x51 NATO, rimless
  (also available in 7.9x57)

Operation Manual, single shots only
Locking system Rotating bolt
Length 1117mm (43.98in)
Weight 4.85kg (10.69lb*) without sights
Barrel 502mm (19.76in), 4 grooves, right-hand twist
Magazine 5-round internal box
Rate of fire NA
Muzzle velocity 850m/sec (2789ft/sec) with standard SS77 ball ammunition

The bolt-action FN-Mauser Model 30-11 rifle is intended for snipers, though this particular example has aperture-type competition sights.

No. 4 Lee-Enfield   Britain

Trials undertaken after the First World War to modernise the venerable Mk III Lee-Enfield rifle, known after 1926 as the Rifle No. 1 Mk 3, resulted in the Mk VI. This had a heavy barrel, a modified body and an improved backsight with distinctive protecting wings; only a few inches of the muzzle protruded from the fore-end. Trials proceeded by way of the No. 1 Mk VI Models B, C and D until the Rifle No. 4 Mk 1 was approved on 15 November 1939.

Though the No. 4 Mk 1 was not issued until the Spring of 1942, most surviving Model B trials rifles were converted to No. 4 standards and issued to the British Army in 1940, shortly after the withdrawal from Dunkirk. Diced fore-ends and fluted handguards distinguish them.

Once the production version of the No. 4 reached service, complaints were made about rough machining and the 6-inch spike bayonet. Many changes were made to fittings during the Second World War to simplify mass production. There were, for example, several No. 4 backsights, and two-groove rifling, approved in 1941, was used until declared obsolete in July 1945. Butt plates on wartime guns were often mazak alloy, stock wood could be inferior, and swivels were reduced to bent wire.

No. 4 Mk 1* Approved in June 1941, made only in Canada and the USA, this had alterations in the action body. The 'catch head, breech bolt' was omitted. Small Arms Ltd of Long Branch, Toronto, made 910,700 Mk 1 and Mk 1* rifles, and the Savage Arms Company of Chicopee Falls, Massachusetts, made 1.236 million (mostly to the Mk 1* pattern).

No. 4 Mk 1/2 A revision of original British-made No. 4 Mk 1 rifles to Mk 2 standards, undertaken from 1949 onward.

No. 4 Mk 1/3 A post-1949 conversion of North American-made No. 4 Mk 1* rifles to Mk 2 standards. Production of Mk 1/2 and Mk 1/3 rifles is believed to have reached 360,000, with all but a few thousand conversions being undertaken in Fazakerley.

No. 4 Mk 1 (T) Approved on 12 February 1942, this was a variant of the No. 4 specially selected for accuracy and issued with No. 32 telescope sights. The No. 32 Mk 1 sight weighed 2lb 3oz, had a 19mm objective lens, a 9-degree field of view, and a range drum graduated 100–1000yd. Most

Soldiers of the Punjab Rifles advance under the cover of a Sherman tank, near Meitkila, Burma, March 1945. They carry No. 1 Lee-Enfield rifles of a pattern that is still held in reserve in India and Pakistan.

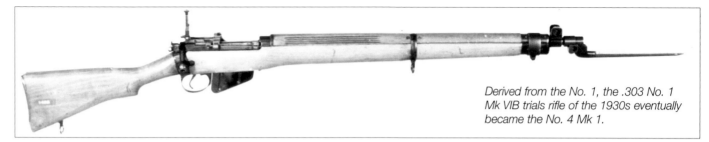

Derived from the No. 1, the .303 No. 1 Mk VIB trials rifle of the 1930s eventually became the No. 4 Mk 1.

of the conversion work was subcontracted to London gunmakers Holland & Holland; BSA-made No. 4 rifles were preferred, though a few Stevens-Savage examples were used in 1942.

No. 4 Mk 2 Approved on 4 December 1947 to replace the unsuccessful No. 5 Jungle Carbine, this was made exclusively in the Enfield factory and introduced to service in 1949. The trigger was mounted on underside of the body instead of on the trigger guard, which prevented the Mk 2 fore-end being exchanged with its predecessors. No. 4 Mk 1 backsights were used.

L8A1 In the 1960s, 7.62mm conversions of the .303 No. 4 Lee-Enfield were developed on the basis of the No. 4 Mk 2. Conversion kits comprising a new barrel, a modified extractor, a new magazine and a charger-guide insert were made in the Royal Small Arms Factory, Enfield (marked 'UE'), and by the Sterling Engineering Co. Ltd of Dagenham ('US').

L8A2 This was based on the No. 4 Mk

1/2, which was itself a conversion to Mk 2 standards of British-made No. 4 Mk I rifles.

L8A3 Based on the No. 4 Mk 1/3, this used North American-made No. 4 actions that had already been modified to Mk 2 standards.

L8A4 A conversion of original unaltered British-made No. 4 Mk 1 rifles, made only in small numbers.

L8A5 Based on the No. 4 Mk 1*, this used unaltered North American-made actions.

L39A1 Touted commercially as the Enfield Envoy and still occasionally seen in service, this has a sporting-style half-stock and aperture sights. Used by the British armed forces for competitive shooting, it is invariably built on a Mk 2 action with the trigger pivoted on the underside of the body.

L42A1 Adopted on 24 August 1970 for issue to British snipers, prior to the introduction of the L96A1 in the mid-1980s, this was converted from existing No. 4 Mk 1 (T) rifles and has the trigger lever pivoted on the trigger guard. It has been issued with

the Telescope, Straight, Sighting, L1A1 – a new designation for the original No. 32 Mk 3 pattern.

Bolt-action rifle: Rifle No. 4 Mk 1
Made by BSA Guns Ltd, Redditch and Shirley, and by the Royal Ordnance Factories in Fazakerley and Maltby, 1940–5

Specification No. 4 Mk 1
  Data from Ian Hogg, *The Greenhill Military Small Arms Data Book* (1999)
Calibre 7.7mm (.303in)
Cartridge 7.7x56, rimmed
Operation Manual, single shots only
Locking system Rotating bolt
Length 1128mm (44.43in)
Weight 4.10kg (9.06lb*) empty
Barrel 522mm (25.19in), 2 or 5 grooves, left-hand twist
Magazine 10-round detachable box
Rate of fire NA
Muzzle velocity 743m/sec (2440ft/sec) with Mk 7 ball ammunition

L1A1 (FN FAL) **Britain**

This shows a Pilkington Pocketscope mounted on a British L1A1 rifle.

Comparative trials undertaken in 1951 with a .280 FN rifle against the EM-2 (Rifle No. 9 Mk 1) favoured the Belgian weapon. A hastily taken decision to adopt the No. 9 was rescinded in October 1952 and 5000 7.62mm FALs were ordered from Fabrique Nationale in 1953. After protracted trials with the experimental X8 series (X8E1–X8E5), work concentrated on the X14E1, with channels cut in the bolt carrier to reduce the likelihood of accumulated fouling jamming the action. By the end of 1956, the British had acquired nearly 15,000 rifles from Fabrique Nationale.

Political wrangling was eventually overcome, and the X14E1 was adopted on 1 March 1957 as the Rifle, 7.62mm, FN, L1A1. Capable only of single-shot fire, the standard infantry rifle is mechanically similar to the Belgian-made prototype (q.v.). It has wooden furniture and a folding cocking handle on the left side of the receiver. Charger guides, tried experimentally, have been omitted from production guns and a longitudinally slotted muzzle brake/compensator is used. Four lengths of butt have been made to suit individual soldiers, and the 30-round L4 (Bren Gun) magazine can be used in an emergency.

British L1A1-type guns have been supplied from Enfield to a selection of Commonwealth and British-aligned countries, including Bangladesh, Belize, Botswana, The Gambia, Ghana, Guyana, Kenya, Mauritius, Sierra Leone, Swaziland, Trinidad & Tobago, and Zambia. Production ceased in the early 1980s.

Auto-loading rifle: Rifle 7.62mm L1A1
Made by the Royal Small Arms Factory, Enfield Lock, Middlesex, and BSA Guns Ltd, Shirley, Warwickshire; *c.* 1958-82

Specification Standard pattern
  Data from Royal Small Arms Factory advertising literature, *L1.A1. Self-Loading Rifle,* undated (c. 1975)
Calibre 7.62mm (.300in)
Cartridge 7.62x51 NATO, rimless
Operation Gas operated, semi-automatic only
Locking system Tipping block
Length 1143mm (45.0in) with standard butt
Weight 4.337kg (9.56lb*) without magazine; 5.074kg (11.19lb*) loaded
Barrel 533.4mm (21.0in), 4 or 6 grooves, right-hand twist
Magazine 20-round detachable box
Rate of fire NA
Muzzle velocity 838m/sec (2750ft/sec) with L2A2 ball rounds

SA80 (L85A1)   Britain

The 5.56mm Infantry Weapon or IW, a bullpup deriving from 4.85mm prototypes, has a multi-lug bolt adapted from the Stoner (ArmaLite) patterns. The perfected 4.85mm guns were publicly unveiled on 14 July 1976, when two rifles and two Light Support Weapons (LSW) were demonstrated.

The standard XL64E5 (ejecting to the right) was entered in NATO trials in 1977, which eventually standardised the 30-round US M16A1 magazine, the French grenade launcher, and the Belgian FN SS109 5.56mm bullet. However, agreement reached among the other participants left the British

4.85mm guns isolated and inspired development of the 5.56mm IW L70E3 (1981), which could be identified by the straight under-edge of the receiver.

The first series-production guns were made in the Enfield factory in 1983 for field trials and issued in the summer of 1984 with the 4x Sight, Unit, Small Arms, Trilux, L9A1 (SUSAT). The shoulder pad, handguard and pistol grip were nylon and the construction relied greatly on stampings, pressings and spot-welding.

L85A1 Adopted in 1985 on the basis of the XL70E3. Compact dimensions and the universal issue of an optical sight have been welcomed, but field service in the Gulf War revealed serious problems attributed more to manufacturing deficiencies and poor-quality ammunition than design faults. The inability of the firer to choose the direction of ejection (cf., French FA MAS) has also been the target of much criticism and the British Army seems unlikely to keep faith with the L85 for much longer.

L98A1 cadet rifle Developed in 1984, this is charged manually by retracting the handle on the right side of the

The original 4.85mm XL64, seen here on trial in 1977, can be distinguished from the perfected 5.56mm patterns by the design of the receiver, which, apart from the magazine housing, was parallel for its length.

breech. The optical sight has been replaced by a pivoting 'L' sight let into the fixed carrying handle. A ten-round magazine was developed specifically for this weapon, though the standard 20- and 30-round IW types can be used when required.

Assault rifle: Individual Weapon (IW), SA-80 or L85
Made by the Royal Small Arms Factory and Royal Ordnance plc, Enfield Lock (to 1988) and Nottingham (1988 to date)

Specification Standard L85A1
   Data from Royal Ordnance advertising literature, *Enfield Weapon System,* dated March 1985
Calibre 5.56mm (.223in)
Cartridge 5.56x45, rimless
Operation Gas operated, selective fire
Locking system Rotating bolt
Length 785mm (30.91in*)
Weight 3.8kg (8.38lb*); empty magazine adds 120g (0.26lb*), plus 800g (1.76lb*) for the optical sight
Barrel 518mm (20.4in*), 6 grooves, right-hand twist
Magazine 30-round detachable box
Rate of fire Not specified (650–800rds/min*)
Muzzle velocity 940m/sec (3084ft/sec*) with M193 ball ammunition

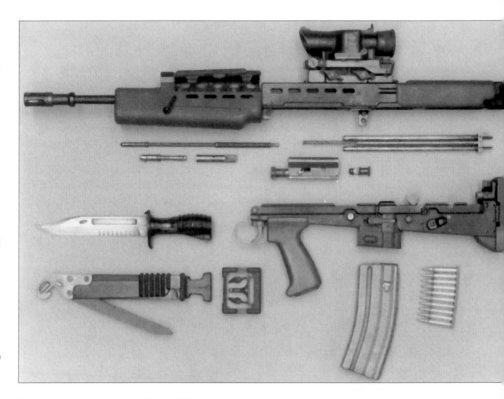

The major components of the 5.56mm L85A1 (SA80) rifle.

Parker-Hale M82 Britain

The Parker-Hale Model 82 sniper rifle was adopted in Australia, Canada and New Zealand. Note the hand-stop beneath the fore-end and the generous use of butt spacers.

The earliest of Parker-Hale's specialised sniper rifles, derived from the company's target-shooting traditions, this has been adopted by Australia and New Zealand – as the Rifle, 7.62mm, Sniper System – and in Canada as the Rifles C3 and C3A1. Antipodean service rifles were customarily fitted with adjustable V-notch backsights in addition to Kahles Helia Zf60 6x42 telescopes; Canadian guns, however, used Kahles Helia or 10x Unertl optical and Parker-Hale PH5E/TX aperture sights interchangeably.

The M82 amalgamates a conventional 1898-type Mauser action with a heavy barrel and an adjustable trigger system contained in a detachable self-contained unit. The safety locks the trigger, bolt and sear simultaneously.

The walnut half-stock may be fitted with a special butt that slides vertically, which allowed large-diameter first generation electro-optical sights to be used in comfort. Spacers can be used to lengthen the butt, and a rail for accessories such as bipods or hand-stops lies under the fore-end.

Bolt-action sniper rifle
Made by Parker-Hale Ltd, Birmingham, 1983–90

Specification Standard pattern
  Data from Ian Hogg, *The Greenhill Military Small Arms Data Book* (1999)
Calibre 7.62mm (.300in)
Cartridge 7.62x51 NATO, rimless
Operation Manual, single shots only
Locking system Rotating bolt
Length 1162mm (45.75in)
Weight 4.80kg (10.56lb*) without sights
Barrel 660mm (25.98in), 4 grooves, right-hand twist
Magazine 4-round internal box
Rate of fire NA
Muzzle velocity 860m/sec (2821ft/sec) with SS77 ball ammunition

Parker-Hale M85   Britain

A camouflaged Parker-Hale M85 sniper rifle, an improved form of the M82 that came close to being adopted in Britain.

This sniper rifle was developed to compete in British Army trials held in the mid-1980s. The detachable box magazine is an improvement on the internal magazine of the preceding Model 82, and the elongated bolt handle (inspired by the Canadian C3A1) facilitates operation if a bulky electro-optical sight has been fitted.

The walnut half-stocks – brown, black or camouflage pattern – are extensively stippled on the pistol grip and fore-end to improve grip. The length of the butt can be adjusted with spacers, and an optional vertically sliding butt section could be fitted to order. A rail let into the underside of the fore-end accepts bipods, hand-stops, sling anchors and similar accessories. A folding rotary aperture sight above the receiver bridge and a protected open blade at the muzzle can be fitted when required.

The British Army assessed the M85 as 'fit for service', but the Accuracy International PM rifle (q.v.) was preferred; however, Parker-Hale sold substantial quantities of Model 85 rifles to police and paramilitary organisations across the world before rights were sold to the Navy Arms Company. Production began in the USA in 1991 in the factory of the Gibbs Rifle Company in Martinsburg, West Virginia.

Bolt-action sniper rifle

Made by Parker-Hale Ltd, Birmingham, 1986–90, and by the Gibbs Rifle Co., Martinsburg, West Virginia, 1991 to date

Specification Standard pattern
Data from manufacturer's handbook, *Parker-Hale 7.62x51mm Sniper Rifle M.85. Operating Information,* dating from October 1985
Calibre 7.62mm (.300in)
Cartridge 7.62x51 NATO
Operation Manual, single shots only
Locking system Rotating bolt
Length 1210mm (47.5in) with all butt spacers fitted
Weight 5.7kg (12.5lb) with optical sight and empty magazine; the bipod adds 670g (1.5lb)
Barrel 698.5mm (27.5in), 4 grooves, right-hand twist
Magazine 10-round detachable box
Rate of fire NA
Muzzle velocity 861m/sec (2825ft/sec) with standard ball ammunition

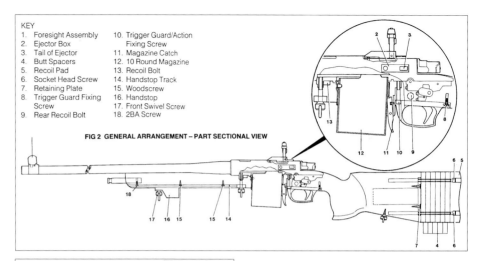

KEY
1. Foresight Assembly
2. Ejector Box
3. Tail of Ejector
4. Butt Spacers
5. Recoil Pad
6. Socket Head Screw
7. Retaining Plate
8. Trigger Guard Fixing Screw
9. Rear Recoil Bolt
10. Trigger Guard/Action Fixing Screw
11. Magazine Catch
12. 10 Round Magazine
13. Recoil Bolt
14. Handstop Track
15. Woodscrew
16. Handstop
17. Front Swivel Screw
18. 2BA Screw

FIG 2 GENERAL ARRANGEMENT – PART SECTIONAL VIEW

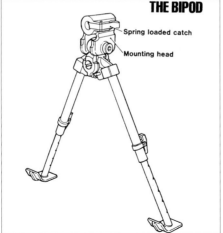

THE BIPOD

Spring loaded catch

Mounting head

Drawings of the Parker-Hale Model 85 rifle and bipod, from the operator's manual.

45

Developed from 1982 onwards by a team led by Malcolm Cooper, and introduced in 1986, the PM has a bolt with 60-degree throw and a fully enclosed head. The barrel screws into an extension of the receiver, where it is held by a collar, and the lugs on the bolt head pass through slots in the collar before turning to lock into place. The use of a barrel collar undoubtedly simplifies construction, and can allow a collar to be replaced if wear increases headspace unacceptably. The action cocks partly on opening and partly on the closing stroke of the bolt; the trigger can be adjusted; and the safety catch blocks trigger, bolt and firing pin simultaneously.

The modular construction pioneered by the PM has become fashionable among the makers of specialised target and precision sniping rifles. Two 'stock sides' – made of tough plastic with black or olive drab finish – are bolted to an aluminium chassis supporting the action, avoiding the warping that occurs when one-piece wood stocks are used in adverse conditions.

The basic rifle is easily recognised by the angularity of its thumbhole half-stock, and by the prominent stock-side retaining bolts; it may also be found with a bipod under the barrel and a small monopod (Quick Action

Spike) beneath the butt. The original PM rifle has now been discontinued in favour of the improved AW pattern, but not before sales were made to more than 20 countries.

PM Counter-Terrorist This has been offered only in 7.62mm NATO chambering, with Schmidt & Bender 6x42 or 2.5-10x56 sights.

PM Covert Derived from the PM Moderated rifle, this can be dismantled into a wheeled suitcase. The most obvious features of the assembled rifle are the pistol grip immediately behind the trigger and a butt which can swing to the left to lie alongside the receiver.

PM Infantry The standard 7.62x51 rifle has a 6x42 Schmidt & Bender optical sight, and often an additional 700yd folding backsight on the receiver above the bolt handle.

PM Long Range Built on a single-shot action, much more rigid that the standard box-magazine design, this gun usually has a 12x42 Schmidt & Bender or 10x/16x Leupold M1 sight, and may chamber 7mm Remington Magnum or .300 Winchester Magnum rounds in search of better accuracy.

PM Moderated This has a 6x42 optical sight and a full-length sound moderator

suited to special subsonic 7.62x51mm ammunition.

PM Super Magnum Developed for the .338 Lapua Magnum cartridge (8.6x70), this rifle can strike with accuracy at longer ranges and also offers better anti-matériel performance. Only a few were made prior to the substitution of the AW-type Super Magnum described below.

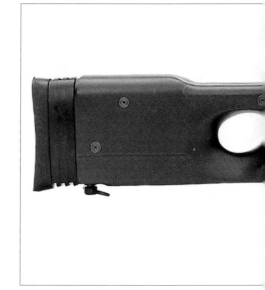

Bolt-action sniper rifle, also known as Model PM
Made for Accuracy International Ltd, Portsmouth, Hampshire, 1986–95

Specification Infantry pattern
Data from a manufacturer's advertising leaflet, *Sniper Rifle Model 'PM'*, dating from *c.* 1987

Calibre 7.62mm (.300in)
Cartridge 7.62x51 NATO, rimless
Operation Manual, single shots only
Locking system Rotating bolt
Length 1124–1194mm (44.25–47.01in*) depending on use of butt spacers
Weight 6.5kg (14.33lb*) with sights and bipod

Barrel Not specified (654mm/25.75in*), 4 grooves, right-hand twist
Magazine 10-round detachable box
Rate of fire NA
Muzzle velocity Not specified (860m/sec, 2821ft/sec, with standard ball ammunition)

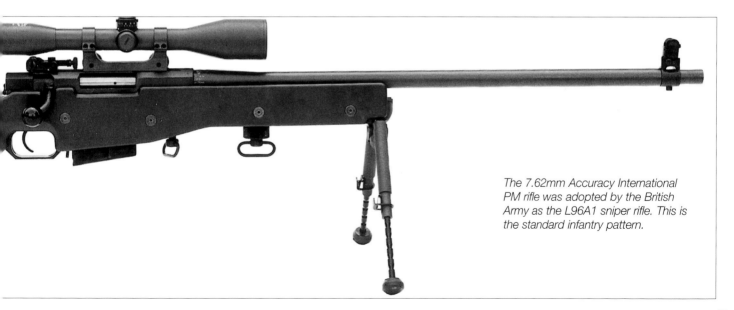

The 7.62mm Accuracy International PM rifle was adopted by the British Army as the L96A1 sniper rifle. This is the standard infantry pattern.

An improved version of the Accuracy International PM sniper rifle, this was developed in 1986–7 for trials in Sweden, where it was eventually adopted as the PSG-90. The bolt action has been improved by changes in the design of individual components, and an anti-icing system allows the rifle to operate reliably in ultra-low temperatures. A three-position safety lever on the right side of the receiver behind the bolt handle can withdraw the firing pin, but the bolt may be locked (full lock) or left free to open (half lock).

A muzzle brake can be attached to the stainless-steel barrel to reduce the recoil sensation, and a modified Parker-Hale QD bipod can be fitted at the tip of the fore-end or to an optional hand-stop on the accessory rail. Open sights can be provided to support the standard Schmidt & Bender Mk II 6x, 10x or 3-12x telescopes, and the rear section of the thumbhole butt can slide vertically to enable the firer to position his eye correctly.

AWP Introduced in 1997 in .243 Winchester or 7.62x51 (.308 Winchester), this Police derivative of the AW has a medium-weight 24in stainless-steel barrel and a 3-12x50 Schmidt & Bender sight.

AWS (suppressed or 'silenced')
Otherwise similar to the standard rifle, this has a full-length sound suppressor and performs best with special subsonic ammunition.

SM, SM-94 or Super Magnum
Resembling the standard AW externally, this chambers the .338 Lapua Magnum cartridge (8.6x70) and has a strengthened six-lug bolt. It is about 1225mm (48.23in*) long with a 686mm (27in) barrel, and weighs 7kg (15.5lb) with sights and bipod. The magazine contains five rounds.

Bolt-action sniper rifle, also known as the Arctic Warfare model
Made for Accuracy International Ltd, Portsmouth, Hampshire, 1992 to date

Specification Standard AW pattern
Data from manufacturer's literature, *Sniper Rifles For Special Forces, Military, Police And Internal Security*, undated (*c.* 1995)
Calibre 7.62mm (.300in)
Cartridge 7.62x51 NATO, rimless
Operation Manual, single shots only
Locking system Rotating bolt
Length 1180mm (46.46in*) approximately
Weight 6.4kg (14.0lb) with sights and bipod

Barrel 660mm (26.0in), 4 grooves, right-hand twist
Magazine 10-round detachable box
Rate of fire NA
Muzzle velocity Not Specified (860m/sec, 2821ft/sec, with standard ball ammunition)

The L96A1 laid the basis for the AW (Arctic Warfare) rifle, adopted by the Swedish armed forces in 1990. This example, lacking open sights, has a Schmidt & Bender 10x42 Mk II optical sight.

The AW rifle in its aluminium case.

C1 (FN FAL)   Canada

The Canadian C1 rifle, distinguished by its disc-type back sight, was just one of many licence-built FAL variants.

The first trials undertaken in 1954 with the experimental EX-1 and EX-2 rifles – with fixed and optical sights respectively – convinced the Canadian authorities of their merits, and the C1 rifle was adopted in June 1955. Unlike the British X14E1 rifle (L1A1), the Canadian variant had charger guides on the receiver and a unique rotating-disc backsight. The furniture was wood, and a cylindrical flash suppressor was fitted.

C1D A selective-fire C1, differing from the army rifle only in the selector and trigger mechanism, this was adopted by the Royal Canadian Navy in 1958.

C1A1 and C1A1D The rigours of service showed that the original firing pin could fail to retract into the breech block automatically if the tip was deformed, igniting the cartridge before the breech was properly locked. The adoption in 1959 of a two-piece firing pin and a new plastic

carrying handle advanced the designation to C1A1 (army) and C1A1D (navy, selective fire). The 7.62mm C1A1 was superseded in 1984 by the 5.56mm C7 rifle, but many large-calibre weapons are still being held in reserve.

C2 This heavyweight pattern, introduced in 1958, shares the mechanism of the C1 but has a combination fore-end/bipod with wood strips attached to the metal legs. The gas tube is exposed above the heavy barrel and a three-position selector lever will be found on the left side of the receiver above the pistol grip. The guns weigh about 6.95kg (15.3lb) with loaded magazines and have sliding-aperture backsights graduated to 1000yd; cyclic rate averages 710rds/min.

C2A1 The introduction of the two-piece firing pin was extended to the C2 in 1960, advancing the designation though only the markings and the plastic carrying handle provide external clues.

Semi-automatic rifle
Made by Canadian Arsenals Ltd, Long Branch, Ontario, 1957–68

Specification Standard fixed-butt C1A1 pattern
Data from John Walter, *Rifles of the World* (second edition, 1998)

Calibre 7.62mm (.300in)
Cartridge 7.62x51 NATO, rimless
Operation Gas operated, semi-automatic fire only
Locking system Tilting block
Length 1136mm* (44.72in)
Weight 4.25kg* (9.37lb) without magazine
Barrel 533mm* (21.0in), 6 grooves, right-hand twist
Magazine 20-round detachable box
Rate of fire NA
Muzzle velocity 838m/sec* (2750ft/sec) with standard ball ammunition

The Canadian Army has now replaced the 7.62mm C1 rifle (FN FAL, q.v.) with the 5.56mm C7, an adaptation of the US M16A2 known to Colt as the Model 715. Developed from a government contract given to Diemaco in the spring of 1983, the C7 is essentially an M16A2 ArmaLite with a simpler pivoting-leaf backsight, a 30-round nylon magazine and a Colt-pattern butt trap. The three-round burst-fire mechanism was discarded in favour of the standard fully automatic setting, and the rifling was optimised to fire SS109 and M193 ammunition with equal facility.

Orders for nearly 80,000 C7 rifles were approved in 1984, the first batches (incorporating Colt-made parts) being delivered in the summer of 1985. The first all-Canadian made gun appeared at the end of 1987. Most of them display 'CANADA/FORCES/CANADIENNES' under a stylised maple leaf on the left side of the magazine housing, above the designation, calibre and serial number. The Diemaco trademark will be found on the left side of the receiver ahead of the selector.

C7A1 This appeared in 1990, with a rail for an optical sight on the receiver top instead of the standard backsight/carrying handle assembly.

C8 This is a compact version of the C7, corresponding to the Colt Model 725, with a short barrel and a telescoping XM177E2-type butt. The first order, for merely 1570 guns, was approved in 1984 but has since been greatly extended.

C8A1 A 1990-vintage variant of the short-barrelled C8 with an optical-sight rail on the receiver. Guns of this type have been purchased by the Special Forces of the Royal Netherlands Army.

Assault rifle
Made by Diemaco Inc., Kitchener, Ontario

Specification Standard fixed-butt pattern Data from Ian Hogg, *The Greenhill Military Small Arms Data Book* (1999)
Calibre 5.56mm (.223in)
Cartridge 5.56x45, rimless
Operation Gas operated, selective fire
Locking system Rotating bolt
Length 1020mm (40.15in)
Weight 3.30kg (7.28lb*)
Barrel 510mm (20.08in*), 6 grooves, right-hand twist
Magazine 30-round detachable box
Rate of fire 800rds/min
Muzzle velocity 925m/sec (3035ft/sec) with standard SS109 ball ammunition

The C7 rifle, shown here under trial in 1986, was a variant of the US M16A2. The first guns were largely made by Colt, but current production is due to Diemaco.

The genesis of this 1963-vintage militia rifle remains uncertain, though at least some of the work has been credited in the Chinese Press to Tang Weng-Li. Though it shares the lines of the SKS (Simonov) carbine, the rotating bolt and piston-type gas system are adaptations of the Kalashnikov. Series production is believed to have begun in 1965.

The Type 63 has a conventional appearance, with a hardwood stock and a machined-steel receiver, but a bayonet pivots on a block beneath the muzzle to lie under the fore-end. The magazine can be loaded through the top of the open action, charger guides being milled into the rear edge of the ejection port. This would be useful in a militia unit armed with a mixture of Type 56 (Simonov) carbines and Type 63 rifles.

Type 68 Introduced in 1969, this has a stamped receiver, minor changes in the action, and a synthetic handguard.

Type 73 Differing from the Types 63 and 68 primarily in the addition of a fully automatic capability, this also uses standard 30-round AK-type magazines.

Type 81 Dating from 1983, this variant of the Type 73 has a three-round burst firing capability instead of the fully automatic setting. It is suspected to have been created for paramilitary or export sales. The Type 81-1 is identical mechanically, but has a folding butt.

Semi-automatic carbine
Made by Factory 90 (?)

Specification Standard Type 68
   Data from Ian Hogg, *The Greenhill Military Small Arms Data Book* (1999)
Calibre 7.62mm (.300in)
Cartridge 7.62x39 M43, rimless
Operation Gas operated, selective fire
Locking system Rotating bolt
Length 1030mm (40.50in)
Weight 3.49kg (7.69lb*) empty
Barrel 521mm (20.50in), 4 grooves, right-hand twist
Magazine 15-round detachable box
Rate of fire 750rds/min
Muzzle velocity 730m/sec (2395ft/sec) with Soviet Type PS ball ammunition

The 7.62mm Type 68 rifle, despite its external resemblance to the SKS, bears more similarity internally to the Kalashnikov.

Vz. 52, Vz. 52/57   Czechoslovakia

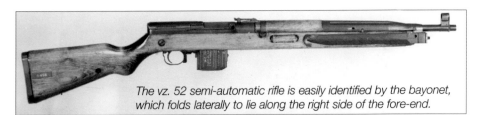

The vz. 52 semi-automatic rifle is easily identified by the bayonet, which folds laterally to lie along the right side of the fore-end.

Formally adopted on 20 March 1952, this was a lightened version of the CZ 502 lacking the gas-regulator system. However, problems with pre-production guns were not solved until a modified prototype (the CZ 521) appeared.

Series production began in 1953, the first guns entering service the following summer. They embodied a tilting-bolt locking system, powered by an annular short-stroke piston, with the locking lugs at the front of the bolt. The action could be loaded through the open action, charger guides being milled in the receiver top. The one-piece pistol-grip stock, made of walnut or beech stained yellow-brown, had a trap in the butt for a cleaning rod, oil can and accessories.

Unfortunately, despite compact dimensions, these rifles were never popular; the cumbersome integral bayonet had an unbalancing effect, and the locking mechanism was found to be unsatisfactory. Vz. 52 and 52/57 guns were withdrawn from the armed forces as soon as the vz. 58 assault rifle became available in quantity. Most of them were subsequently sold to countries that were then sympathetic to communism – e.g., Egypt, Syria, Cuba and Nicaragua – and survivors are still to be found in the hands of militiamen and guerrilla groups throughout Africa.

Vz. 52/57 Unification of the weapons of the Soviet-bloc states was agreed in 1954, prior to the signing of the Warsaw Pact. Pressure applied by the USSR forced the Czechoslovakian authorities to alter the vz. 52 for the 7.62x39 M43 Soviet intermediate cartridge. The modified rifles are sighted to 900m for the slower Russian-style bullet, weigh about 4.3kg empty, and have magazines with distinctively sloped base plates. Some guns appear to have been newly made, but others were converted from 7.62x45.

Semi-automatic carbine: 7.62mm samonabijecki puška vz. 52
Made by Československá Zbrojovka, Uhersky Brod (code 'tgf')

Specification vz. 52
   Data from Ian Hogg, *The Greenhill Military Small Arms Data Book* (1999)
Calibre 7.62mm (.300in)
Cartridge 7.62x45, rimless
Operation Gas operated, semi-automatic fire only
Locking system Tilting bolt
Length 1015mm (40.0in) with bayonet folded
Weight 4.08kg (9.0lb) empty
Barrel 520mm (20.5in), 4 grooves, right-hand twist
Magazine 10-round detachable box
Rate of fire NA
Muzzle velocity 743m/sec (2440ft/sec) with Czechoslovakian Z 50 ball ammunition

This design of this weapon was inspired by a competition held in 1953 to find a Kalashnikov-type assault rifle for the Czechoslovakian Army, field trials being undertaken with the ZK 503, ČZ 522 and ZB 530. The trials resolved in favour of the Holek (ZB) design, but work was deferred while the mechanism was adapted for the 7.62mm Soviet M43 cartridge by Josef Čermak.

Full-scale production of the Samopal vz. 58/P (*pechotni,* infantry) began in 1958. Though superficially resembling the Kalashnikov, it has a tilting-block locking system and an axial striker instead of a swinging hammer. The selector can be found on the right side of the receiver above the pistol grip.

The vz. 58/V assault rifle (left), *chambering the Soviet 7.62mm M43 cartridge, has a butt that folds laterally to the right. The standard infantry version, vz. 58/P* (right), *has a fixed butt.*

The earliest guns had wooden butts, pistol grips and fore-ends, but reddish-brown plastic/wood-fibre composites had been substituted by *c.* 1962. The newest guns, dating from the 1970s, have nylon polymer fittings. The external finish was usually phosphating, though guns have been seen with baked-on grey-green paint.

Vz. 58/V Used by armoured and airborne units, this had a single-strut metal butt folding to the right alongside the receiver.

Assault rifle: Samopal 58/P
Made by Ceskoslovenská Zbrojovka, Povaske Strjirny (code 'she')

Specification Standard infantry version
Data from Ian Hogg, *The Greenhill Military Small Arms Data Book* (1999)
Calibre 7.62mm (.300in)
Cartridge 7.62x39 M43, rimless
Operation Gas operated, selective fire
Locking system Tilting block
Length 843mm (33.20in)
Weight 3.11kg (6.88lb*) (without magazine)
Barrel 400mm (15.80in), 4 grooves, right-hand twist
Magazine 30-round detachable box
Rate of fire 800rds/min
Muzzle velocity 710m/sec (2330ft/sec) with Soviet PS ball ammunition

ČZ 2000

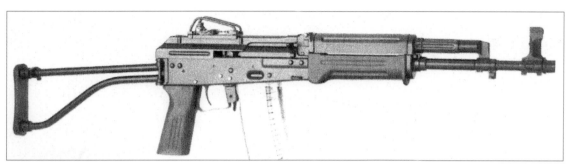

The ČZ 2000 or LADA assault rifle awaits funding before it can be adopted by the army of the Czech Republic.

Part of a weapons system developed in the Uhersky Brod factory in the early 1990s, this gun was introduced in 1995, though long-term success awaits a decision to re-equip the Czech Army. The action derives from the Kalashnikov, and has a modified AKM-type breech cover retained by a cross-pin. A four-position selector on the left side of the receiver can be set, in addition to the locked or safe position, to give automatic fire ('30'), three-round bursts controlled by a pawl-and-ratchet mechanism ('3') or single shots ('1').

The pistol grip, fore-end and barrel guard are all made of styrene foam reinforced with fibreglass, and the backsight lies within two sturdy steel-wire protectors. Feed may be from a conventional box magazine or a 75-round drum. The ČZ

2000, which can alternatively be configured as a carbine or a light machine-gun, may have a fixed butt or a folding pattern that can be swung to the right alongside the receiver. The standard finish is black phosphating.

ČZ 2000 carbine A short-barrelled assault rifle, with a conical flash-hider/muzzle brake instead of the longer slotted type, this is 675mm (26.75in long) with the butt extended, has a 185mm (7.28in) barrel, and weighs 2.6kg (5.75lb*).

Assault rifle: also known as LADA
Made by Česká Zbrojovka, Uhersky Brod

Specification Standard infantry version
  Data from Ian Hogg, *The Greenhill Military Small Arms Data Book* (1999)
Calibre 5.56mm (.223in)
Cartridge 5.56x45, rimless (also made in 5.45x39 M74)
Operation Gas operated, selective-fire only
Locking system Rotating bolt
Length 850mm (33.46in)
Weight 3.0kg (6.56lb*) empty
Barrel 382mm (15.04in), 6 grooves, right-hand twist
Magazine 30-round detachable box
Rate of fire 800rds/min
Muzzle velocity 910m/sec (2985ft/sec) with SS109 ball ammunition

Hakim   Egypt

The 7.9x57 Hakim rifle, an adaptation of the Swedish Ljungmann, was found wanting in the desert and was speedily replaced by a licence-built Kalashnikov.

Fabrique Nationale supplied the Egyptian Army with substantial quantities of 7.9x57mm SAFN rifles in the days of King Farouk, but these were rapidly replaced by the Hakim. Based on the Swedish Ljungmann rifle, production began in 1955 with the assistance of machine tools purchased from Husqvarna.

The rifle is essentially similar to the Swedish AG.42B, sharing the straight-tube gas system and breech-cover cocking system, but was much more robust and the size of the gas port could be adjusted to handle variations in ammunition pressure. The pistol-grip stock ran to the muzzle, with a wooden handguard from the chamber to the nose cap. A perforated muzzle brake/compensator appeared ahead of the front-sight block.

Egyptian service weapons will display Arabic numbers on the backsight leaf, and are usually dated on the front left side of the receiver above the serial number. Combat experience showed the Hakim to be acceptably accurate, but also that it was far too heavy and made to such fine tolerances that the desert sand readily jammed it. The Egyptians rapidly substituted the lighter and more reliable Kalashnikov, commencing work in Factory 54 (with Russian help) in the late 1950s.

Rashid Apparently dating from the period in which tooling for the Kalashnikov was being undertaken, this improved Hakim retained the direct-impingement gas system. However, the charging handle was attached directly to the bolt carrier and an SKS-type bayonet pivoted on an attachment block behind the front sight.

Auto-loading rifle
Made by the State Factory 54, Port Said (later Maadi Military & Civil Industries Company)

Specification Standard version
Data from Ian Hogg, *The Greenhill Military Small Arms Data Book* (1999)
Calibre 7.9mm (.311in)
Cartridge 7.9x57, rimless
Operation Gas operated, semi-automatic fire only
Locking system Tilting bolt
Length 1209mm (47.60in)
Weight 4.82kg (10.63lb*) empty
Barrel 590mm (23.23in), 4 grooves, right-hand twist
Magazine 10-round detachable box
Rate of fire NA
Muzzle velocity 870m/sec (2854ft/sec)

The 7.62x39 Rashid rifle was a derivative of the Hakim, but was never more than a stopgap.

The 7.62mm Rynakkokivääri m/62 TP (folding-stock version), with its distinctive knife bayonet.

The first prototypes of the improved Kalashnikov were made in the mid-1950s, with the m/58 Valmet prototype laying the basis for the perfected designs. This was succeeded by the semi-experimental m/60, one pattern being developed by Valmet and another by Sako. The best features of the two rivals were then combined in the m/62. The receiver was simplified, the ribbed plastic handguard varied, and the pistol grip took different forms.

The furniture was a dark-greenish hue on the original Sako-made examples, but black on the later Valmet examples. The gas tube of the original guns generally lay in a stamped liner, with the top exposed, while later ones were often enclosed. The backsight attachment was improved in the late 1960s, when a solid-top hood replaced the previous open pattern. Selectors were marked • (single shots) and ••• (automatic fire), the dots being impressed on early guns but raised on later examples. Serial numbers of Valmet-made guns began at 100001, whereas Sako products commenced at 200001.

m/62, new pattern From 1972 onward,

tritium night sights were fitted to new guns and the rounded backsight protectors were replaced by taller square versions. Rifles with the original sights were then reclassified as m/62 PT. After purchasing small numbers of the m/62/76 *(see below)*, the Finns returned to the folding-butt m/62 in 1985 on the grounds that the machined-steel receiver was more durable than the stamped version. Orders for about 40,000 new guns had been placed with the Sako-Valmet combine by the end of 1988.

m/62 PT A post-1972 designation applied retrospectively to m/62 rifles with the original sights.

Assault rifle: Rynakkokivääri m/62
Made by Valmet Oy, Jyväskylä, 1963–75;
and Oy Sako Ab, Riihimäki, 1963–6

Specification Standard m/62
  Data from Ian Hogg, *The Greenhill
  Military Small Arms Data Book* (1999)
Calibre 7.62mm (.300in)
Cartridge 7.62x39 M43, rimless
Operation Gas operated, selective fire

Locking system Rotating bolt
Length 914mm (36.0in)
Weight 4.09kg (9.0lb) with empty
  magazine
Barrel 419mm (16.50in), 4 grooves,
  right-hand twist
Magazine 30-round detachable box
Rate of fire 650rds/min
Muzzle velocity 730m/sec (2400ft/sec)
  with Soviet PS ball ammunition

*A Finnish soldier on manoeuvres takes aim
with his m62 assault rifle. Note that this
gun has a fixed tubular butt.*

Rynakkokivääri m/76

Service experience showed that the Finnish m/62/76 assault rifle was not as durable as the original m/62, owing to changes made in its construction.

A series of Valmet prototypes was followed by the m/76, introduced in 1977 with a sheet-steel receiver. A few rifles of this type were purchased by the Finnish armed forces, but did not prove durable enough to displace the m/62. The basic rifle has, however, been sold in quantity to Qatar and Indonesia. A variety of commercial selective-fire patterns has been made, including the guns with folding tubular butts (76F), fixed plastic butts (76P), fixed tubular butts (76T) and fixed wooden butts (76W).

m/62/76 This is the Finnish Army designation for the standard rifle, with a selector (safe, single-shot and fully automatic positions) on the right side of the receiver.

m/62/76 TP The standard folding-butt *(Taittoperä)* variant.

m/82 (Model 76B) Introduced by Valmet in 1981, this was a bullpup version of the Model 76. The standard action was inserted in a one-piece synthetic stock, considerably reducing overall length. The trigger and pistol grip were moved forward ahead of the magazine, and a special raised backsight lay ahead of the ejection port. The gun was extensively tested by the Finnish Army, but was never accepted.

Assault rifle: Rynakkokivääri m/62/76
Made by Valmet Corporation, Defence Equipment Group, Jyväskylä, 1976–88, and Sako-Valmet, 1988–90

Specification Standard m/76 TP
  Data from a manufacturer's advertising leaflet, *Valmet Automatic Rifles 5.56 and 7.62*, dated 1985
Calibre 5.56mm (.223in); also available in 7.62mm
Cartridge 5.56x45, rimless
Operation Gas operated, selective fire
Locking system Rotating bolt
Length 950mm (37.40in*) with butt extended, 710mm (27.95in*) with butt folded
Weight 3.90kg (8.60lb*) without magazine; loaded 30-round magazine, 620g (1.37lb*)
Barrel 420mm (16.54in*), 6 grooves, right-hand twist
Magazine 15-, 20- or 30-round detachable box
Rate of fire 600rds/min
Muzzle velocity 975m/sec (3199ft/sec*) with M193 ball ammunition

Rynakkokiväari m/95   Finland

The experimental Sako m/90 assault rifle was adapted to become the Finnish m/95 TP.

On 1 January 1987, Sako and Valmet amalgamated as Sako-Valmet Oy. After several changes in the controlling interests, the Sako name was bestowed on a privately capitalised company making rifles and ammunition in the Riihimäki and Jyväskylä factories respectively.

Development of a new assault rifle had already begun, though the first prototypes (known tentatively as the m/90) dated only from 1989–90. Considerable changes were made to the selector, which was moved to the left side of the receiver. A spring-loaded cover plate was added to prevent snow and dust entering the charging-handle slot, and improvements were made internally.

The Finnish Defence Force decided that interchangeability with the existing m/62 and m/62/76 rifles had been compromised, and so the simpler m/92/62 was eventually adopted as the m/95 TP. The guns have a tubular butt that can swing forward alongside the receiver, changes in the housing give additional support to the magazine, and a rail for optical and electro-optical sights has been added on the left side of the receiver. The charging handle tips upward so that it can be retracted with the left hand. Tritium 'dusk sights' and an improved muzzle brake/compensator have been adopted, but the end of assault-rifle production in Finland in 1997 ensures that the m/95 will never be made in quantity.

Assault rifle: Rynakkokiväari m/95
Made by Sako-Valmet, Riihimäki, 1995–7

Specification m/90 prototype
  Data from Sako advertising literature dated 1991
Calibre 7.62mm (.300in); also available in 5.56mm
Cartridge 7.62x39 M43, rimless
Operation Gas operated, selective fire
Locking system Rotating bolt
Length 930mm (36.61in*) with butt extended; 675mm (26.57in*) with butt folded
Weight 3.85kg (8.49lb*) without magazine; empty 30-round plastic magazine, 160g (5.6oz*)
Barrel 416mm (16.38in*), 4 grooves, right-hand twist
Magazine 30-round detachable box
Rate of fire 600–750rds/min
Muzzle velocity Not specified
  (c. 710m/sec, 2329ft/sec, with Soviet PS ball ammunition)

Sako TRG-21   Finland

Built on a standard Sako action, the TRG-21 is easily distinguished by the free-floating barrel and a synthetic half-stock attached to an aluminium-alloy frame. The butt can be lengthened with spacers, whilst the height and rake of the comb can be adjusted by altering the cheek piece.

The receiver rail will accept mounts for optical and electro-optical sights, though folding open sights are provided for emergency use. The trigger can be adjusted for release pressure

(2.2–5.5lb), and the trigger lever can be moved to suit an individual grip. The safety catch – which locks the trigger, bolt and firing pin – lies inside the trigger guard. Most guns have bipods fixed to the front of the stock frame, and the combination muzzle brake/flash hider is threaded to accept a sound-suppressor.

TRG-41 This is simply a TRG-21 chambered for the .338 Lapua Magnum cartridge, with a magazine capacity restricted to five rounds.

Bolt-action sniper rifle
Made by Oy Sako Ab, Riihimäki

Specification Standard pattern
  Data from Ian Hogg, *The Greenhill Military Small Arms Data Book* (1999)
Calibre 7.62mm (.300in)
Cartridge 7.62x51 NATO, rimless
Operation Manual, single shots only
Locking system Rotating bolt
Length 1150mm (45.28in)
Weight 4.7kg (10.36lb*) without sights
Barrel 660mm (26.0in), 4 grooves, right-hand twist
Magazine 10-round detachable box
Rate of fire NA
Muzzle velocity 860m/sec (2821ft/sec) with standard SS77 ball ammunition

The Sako TRG-21 sniper rifle in its silenced guise.

MAS 36   France

The 7.5x54 MAS 36 CR39 rifle, with its unique folding butt, was designed for French paratroops.

The introduction in 1924 of a rimless 7.5mm cartridge, which was far better ballistically than the venerable 8mm rimmed pattern, forced the French to re-examine their infantry weapons. Prototypes were offered from Tulle and Saint-Étienne in the late 1920s. Virtually all had charger-loaded magazines, and socket or spike bayonets that could be reversed into the fore-end when not required.

The MAT 1932 rifle had a two-piece stock and a simple bolt with the operating handle bent forward so that its ball lay immediately above the trigger guard. Development of the MAT 1932 then produced the MAS 34, the B1 version being accepted for service in 1935 as the MAS 36.

The pistol-grip butt was separated from the fore-end and handguard by a massive forged receiver containing the one-piece bolt, though simplicity was taken to such extremes that no manual safety catch was fitted. The backsight lay on the rear of the receiver, immediately ahead of the firer's eye. A machined nose cap carried the front sight, with a spike-type bayonet in a channel in the fore-end and a stacking rod protruding from the right side of the cap.

The first deliveries were made in 1937, but few MAS 36 rifles had reached the army when the Germans invaded France in 1940. The metal parts of these pre-war guns were generally phosphated, though some were apparently painted black – perhaps those made hurriedly in 1939–40 – and others were browned for the navy and marines.

Production began again in 1945, post-war guns embodying a tunnel-pattern front-sight protector and sheet-metal mounts. The backsight was modified so that the adjustment rack lay on the sight base instead of the leaf.

MAS 36 CR 39 Adopted for airborne infantry and alpine ski-troops in 1939, this was simply a short MAS 36 with a bifurcated aluminium butt which could be folded forward around the trigger and lower part of the receiver.

MAS 36 LG 48 Some guns were modified in the late 1940s to accept the 1948-type grenade launcher. These had a folding sight-arm on the left side of a new machined-steel nose cap with an 'eared' front-sight protector. Grenade range was varied by rotating a collar around the muzzle.

MAS 36 LG 51 Approval of a NATO-standard grenade launcher allowed some rifles to be modified in 1952–5. These had an elongated ribbed muzzle and a pivoting grenade-sight arm set into the top upper part of the handguard. A few guns were chambered for .30-06 or 7.62mm NATO cartridges, but 7.5x54mm remained standard.

Bolt-action rifle: Fusil MAS 36
Made by Manufacture d'Armes de Saint-Étienne

Specification Standard pattern
Data from Ian Hogg, *The Greenhill Military Small Arms Data Book* (1999)
Calibre 7.5mm (0.295in)
Cartridge 7.5x54mm, rimless.
Operation Manual, single shots only
Locking system Rotating bolt
Length 1020mm (40.15in)
Weight 3.85kg (8.33lb*) empty
Barrel 573mm (22.60in), 4 grooves, left-hand twist
Magazine 5-round internal charger-loaded box
Rate of fire NA
Muzzle velocity 823m/sec (2700ft/sec) with *Balle* 1929 C

MAS Mle 49/56   France

A typical MAS Mle 49/56.

The introduction of rimless cartridges in the 1920s encouraged experimentation with semi-automatic rifles and allowed a series of prototypes to be made in the government factory in Saint-Étienne between the wars. The earliest designs were based on the Mle 1918 RSC, whereas the MAS 39 was similar to the Soviet Tokarev. Work began in the autumn of 1944 to perfect the MAS 39 rifle for series production, the first trial batches of MAS 44 rifles being delivered in 1946 to marine commandos in Indo-China.

The rifle shared the two-piece stock, fittings, bayonet and magazine of the bolt-action MAS 36, but had a deep receiver containing the breech block and carrier assembly. The cocking handle protruded from the front right side of the feed way and the backsight lay in front of the firer's eye.

Next came the MAS 44-A of 1948, developed to fire grenades, and production

of the perfected MAS 49 began in Saint-Étienne in 1951. The action relied on gas tapped from the top of the barrel to impinge directly on the bolt carrier; as the carrier began to move back, it lifted the rear of the breech block above the locking shoulder in the receiver and the whole mechanism reciprocated to reload the chamber. The gas tube of the MAS 49 was bent to follow the contours of the barrel, allowing weight to be saved in the fore-end and handguard; empty weight was 3.93kg.

Production of the MAS 49/56 commenced in 1957. The rifle could fire NATO-type rifle grenades, as a special sight was pivoted to the back of the front-sight mounting block and the launcher collar/muzzle brake had a standardised diameter of 22mm. The butt was the same as the earlier pattern, but the fore-end and handguard were shortened to accommodate the grenade-launcher sight.

Accessories included the Mle 1953 telescope sight, a rubber cheek piece, and rubber butt plates.

MAS 49/56 SN About 250 rifles destined for security police (*Sûreté Nationale*) were converted in the mid-1960s to fire 7.62x51mm NATO ammunition, the grenade launcher being modified to fire tear gas and baton rounds.

Semi-automatic rifle: Fusil automatique MAS 49/56
Made by Manufacture d'Armes de Saint-Étienne

Specification Standard version
   Data from Ian Hogg, *The Greenhill Military Small Arms Data Book* (1999)
Calibre 7.5mm (.295in)
Cartridge 7.5x54mm, rimless
Operation Gas operated, automatic fire only
Locking system Rotating bolt
Length 1022mm (40.23in)
Weight 3.88kg (8.5lb) empty
Barrel 580mm (22.83in), 4 grooves, left-hand twist
Magazine 10-round detachable box
Rate of fire NA
Muzzle velocity 838m/sec (2749ft/sec) with Mle 29C ball ammunition

The 5.56mm FA MAS is a very compact design. Note the bipod folded back along the fore-end beneath the carrying handle.

The first prototypes of this idiosyncratic bullpup rifle were exhibited at Satory in June 1973, though design work had hardly been completed. The perfected A3 prototypes were issued for field trials in 1976, series production began in 1979, and the first issues reached the French Army early in 1980. No positive lock is used, the mechanism relying on pivoting transverse levers connecting the bolt and bolt carrier to delay the opening of the breech until chamber pressure drops to a safe level.

Known colloquially as *Le Clairon* (Bugle), the FA MAS cannot be mistaken for any other gun, owing to its ultra-compact dimensions and the unusually long carrying handle. The bipod folds back along the sides of the receiver, above the pistol grip, and the direction of ejection can be changed simply by altering the position of the extractor on the bolt and reversing the cheek piece. The action is charged by a handle on top of the receiver, beneath the carrying handle.

Packaged in a replaceable synthetic box, the trigger system relied on a ratchet escapement to fire three-shot bursts. The selector in the trigger guard could be moved from 'S' (*sûr*, safe) to '1' for single shots. With the main selector set to 'R' and the burst-fire selector under the trigger on '0', the FA MAS would fire fully automatically; if the settings were 'R' and '3', a three-round burst ensued.

The rifle has been successful enough to satisfy the authorities and has been popular in army service, though claims have been made that the delayed blowback system is only marginally effective if high-pressure 5.56mm cartridge are used, and thus that extraction failures will occur even though the chamber is fluted.

FA MAS G2 Adopted by the French Navy in 1995, and then by the army, this is an improved version of the original rifle (retrospectively designated G1) with an enlarged trigger guard, a more robust breech-block buffer, a NATO-standard magazine interface, and a lipped fore-end to constrain the firer's hand. The rifling is a compromise design, making a turn in 228mm (8.97in) so that it can fire M193 and SS109 ball ammunition interchangeably.

Assault rifle: Fusil d'Assaut MAS (FA MAS)
Made by Manufacture d'Armes, de Saint-Étienne (subsequently part of Groupement Industriel des Armements Terrestres [GIAT], Saint-Cloud)

Specification Standard version
Data from Ian Hogg, *The Greenhill Military Small Arms Data Book* (1999)
Calibre 5.56mm (.223in)
Cartridge 5.56x45mm, rimless.
Operation Delayed blowback, selective fire
Locking system Inertia of two-part bolt/bolt carrier assembly suffices
Length 757mm (29.8in)
Weight 3.61kg (7.96lb*) with bipod and empty magazine
Barrel 488mm (19.2in), 3 grooves, right-hand twist
Magazine 25-round detachable box
Rate of fire 900–1000rds/min
Muzzle velocity 960m/sec (3150ft/sec) with standard M193 ball ammunition

The FA MAS on ceremonial duty, showing the inverted position of the fixed bayonet.

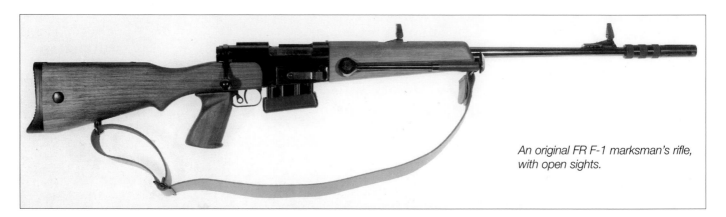

An original FR F-1 marksman's rifle, with open sights.

This sniper rifle, introduced in 1964, was developed from the MAS 36 by the factory design bureau and a leading French rifleman, Jean Fournier. The military FR F-1 Type A or *Tireur d'Élite* has a distinctive wood butt with a shallow pistol grip, a separate hand grip immediately behind the trigger, and an enveloping fore-end from which the slender floating barrel protrudes. A bipod and a muzzle brake were usually fitted.

Wooden spacers could be used to lengthen the butt, and two differing detachable synthetic cheek pieces could be obtained. A lever-pattern magazine catch lay on the right side of the receiver, and the magazine was generally fitted with a detachable rubber cover.

French Army rifles were usually accompanied by the 3.8x Mle 1953 L.806 optical sight, though guns used by the French national police and anti-terrorist agencies prefer 1.5-6x Zeiss Diavari patterns.

FR F-2 Introduced in 1984 and offered only in 7.62x51mm, this has a sturdier bipod on a yoke around the barrel (immediately ahead of the receiver) and a plastic-coated metal frame serving as a fore-end. A plastic sleeve encloses the barrel to minimise the effects of radiated heat on the sight picture and reduce the risk of infra-red detection.

FR-G1 A variant of the FR-F2, intended for export, this lacks the thermal sleeve. The fore-end has reverted to the traditional wooden pattern, and the bipod legs cannot be adjusted.

FR-G2 Otherwise identical with the G1 version, this had a bipod with adjustable legs.

*Sniper rifle: Fusil à Répétition,
Modèle F-1*
Made by Manufacture d'Armes, de Saint-
Étienne (subsequently part of
Groupement Industriel des Armements
Terrestres [GIAT], Versailles-Satory)

Specification Rifle Type A
  Data from Ian Hogg, *The Greenhill
  Military Small Arms Data Book* (1999)
Calibre 7.5mm (.295in)
Cartridge 7.5x54, rimless (7.62x51
  NATO optional)
Operation Manual, single shots only
Locking system Rotating bolt
Length 1138mm (44.80in)
Weight 5.20kg (11.44lb*) with bipod and
  empty magazine
Barrel 552mm (21.73in) excluding
  muzzle brake, 4 grooves, right-hand
  twist
Magazine 10-round detachable box
Rate of fire NA
Muzzle velocity 852m/sec (2795ft/sec)

*The FR F-1 rifle in action, 1992. This is a
later version than the gun in the preceding
picture, with a modified bipod, a muzzle
brake, and a schnabel-tip fore-end.*

Introduced in 1935, the *Karabiner 98k* was a short rifle version of the 1898-pattern Mauser infantry rifle of the First World War. The basic action remained identical, but a tangent-leaf backsight was fitted. There was a single barrel band, and the H-type nose cap was accompanied by a 4cm bayonet bar beneath the muzzle. The sling-attachment consisted of a slot in the butt and a short fixed bar on the left side of the barrel band.

Manufacturing standards fell as the fighting progressed, creating the so-called 'War Model' *(Kriegsmodell)* of 1942. Distinguishing characteristics included stamped nose caps, barrel bands and butt-plates, crudely finished trigger-guards and thinly varnished stocks. Most guns – but by no means all – had laminated stocks, the result of trials that had stretched through the 1930s. Plywood laminates resisted warping better than the conventional

one-piece patterns, did not require lengthy maturing, and were less wasteful.

***Zielfernrohr-Karabiner* 98k (Zf-Kar 98k)** Introduced in 1941 and identical with the Kar 98k apart from sights, these were selected for their accuracy. Early combinations used 4x Zf 39 sights made by Zeiss, Leitz, Goerz, Hensoldt and others; during the war, however, smaller 1.5x Zf 40, 41, 41/1 and 41/2 long eye-relief patterns became common. Zf 39 had separate 'turret' mounts, on top of

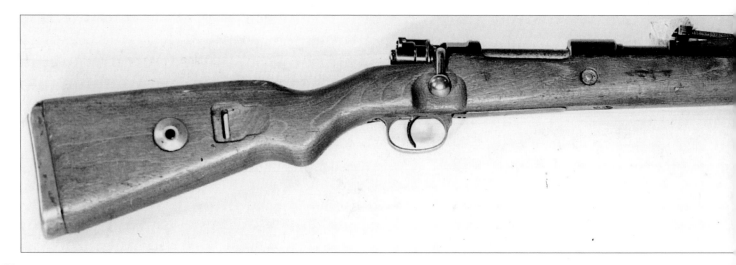

the receiver bridge and the chamber, or (more rarely) a one-piece twin ring mount clamped on to a rail on the left side of the receiver; 1.5x sights were held by a sprung latch to a rail on the backsight. A few guns dating from 1944–5 used the stubby Zf 4 sight, developed for the Gew 43, in a rearward-slanting twin-ring monoblock. Due to mass manufacturing of the Kar 98k before 1945, thousands served in the post-war period.

Bolt-action rifle: Karabiner 98k
Made by Mauser-Werke AG, Oberndorf am Neckar, Württemberg (code 'S/42', '42', 'byf' or 'svw'); Mauser-Werke AG, Berlin-Borsigwalde ('S/243', '243' or 'ar'); Sauer & Sohn, Suhl ('S/147', '147' or 'ce'); Berlin-Lübecker Maschinenfabrik, Lübeck ('S/237' or '237'); Waffenwerk Brünn AG, Brno ('dot'); Fabrique Nationale d'Armes de Guerre, Herstal-lèz-Liége ('ch'); Feinmechanische Werke GmbH, Erfurt ('S/27', '27' and 'ax');

Gustloff-Werke, Weimar ('bcd'); and Steyr-Daimler-Puch AG, Steyr/Oberdonau ('660', 'bnz')

Specification Standard pattern
    Data from Karl Fischer, *Waffen- und Schiesstechnischer Leitfaden für die Ordnungspolizei* (fifth edition, 1944)
Calibre 7.9mm (.311in)
Cartridge 7.9x57mm, rimless.
Operation Manual, single-shots only
Locking system Rotating bolt
Length 1110mm (43.70in*)
Weight 3.9kg (8.60lb*) empty
Barrel 600mm (23.62in*), 4 grooves, right-hand twist
Magazine 5-round internal charger-loaded box
Rate of fire NA
Muzzle velocity 755m/sec (2477ft/sec*) with S-*Patrone*

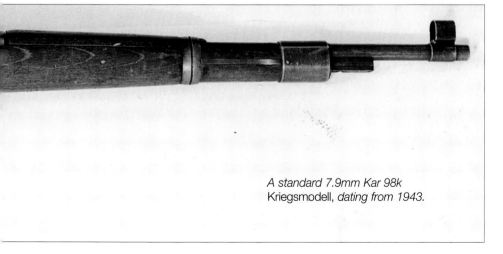

A standard 7.9mm Kar 98k Kriegsmodell, dating from 1943.

The MKb 42 (H) was the prototype of the first successful assault rifle.

Though the rival Walther prototype, the MKb 42 (W), was lighter, better balanced and more accurate, the simpler Haenel was easier to make in quantity. It was adopted in 1943 once an adaptation of the Walther hammer-fired trigger mechanism had replaced the original striker. The finalised rifle also fired from a closed breech.

The MP 43 of 1943 was the first weapon of its type to be mass-produced. Relying on an untried subcontract system, work did not always proceed smoothly; many of the components made by outworkers had to be hand-finished to fit and deliveries were erratic. Consequently, its influence on post-war thinking was appreciably greater than its contribution to the campaign history of the Second World War.

MP 43 This had a ball-tipped rod projecting from the gas-port assembly instead of the original extended gas tube.

MP 43/1 The muzzle of these guns was modified to accept a special grenade launcher (MP GwGrGt 43); most other versions had a short muzzle for the Kar 98k-type launcher. Most MP 43/1 and some MP 44 rifles had side-rails accepting the Zf 4 optical sight or the *Zielgerät* 1229 *Vampir* night sight.

MP 44 The basic gun was renamed in 1944 to emphasise the beginning of mass production, though no modifications had been made.

StG 44 The MP 44 was eventually renamed *Sturmgewehr* 44 (StG 44) in recognition of its capabilities.

Assault rifle: Maschinenpistole 43, MP 43
Made by C.G. Haenel Waffen- und Fahrradfabrik (code 'fxo'), Suhl; and by Erfurter Maschinenfabrik B. Geipel GmbH 'Erma-Werk' ('ayf'), Erfurt. Mauser-Werke AG ('byf') of Oberndorf

and an unidentified company using the code 'sup' made receivers, and many lesser contractors were involved in the supply of components

Specification Standard MP 43
  Data from Ian Hogg, *The Greenhill Military Small Arms Data Book* (1999)
Calibre 7.9mm (.311in)
Cartridge 7.9x33 *Kurz-Patrone*
Operation Gas operated, selective fire

Locking system Tilting bolt
Length 940mm (37in)
Weight 5.12kg (11.25lb*) (with empty magazine?)
Barrel 418mm (16.50in), 4 grooves, right-hand twist
Magazine 30-round detachable box
Rate of fire 500rds/min
Muzzle velocity 647m/sec (2125ft/sec) with standard ball cartridges

The 7.9x33 MP 43, known by a variety of designations, was the world's first successful assault rifle. This captured example is being examined by a senior British officer.

Heckler & Koch G3   Germany

This photograph shows a first-generation Heckler & Koch G3 rifle, with a metal fore-end, and a first-generation Eltro-Zeiss Orion 80 electro-optical sight.

A promising trial of the Spanish CETME (q.v.) rifle was undertaken in Germany in 1955, and, after the action had been revised for the US .30 T65 cartridge (later 7.62x51 NATO), the German defence ministry ordered about 400 for trials in 1956 – apparently through Heckler & Koch, though the guns were made in Spain. Tests were satisfactory, but many changes were requested and the finalised German-made gun fired from a closed bolt.

In 1958, the licence granted by CETME to the Dutch NWM organisation was transferred to Heckler & Koch whilst enough B-type CETME rifles were purchased to allow field trials to begin in

Germany in 1959. The first-pattern German rifle was approved for service in 1960, replacing the *Gewehr 1* (FAL). It had a rocking-'L' backsight (*Klappvisier*), a bipod and a folding carrying handle. The improved G3 appeared in 1963, with a drum sight (*Drehvisier*) which rotated around a steeply inclined axis ahead of the firer's eye. The bipod and carrying handle were abandoned.

The G3 is made largely of pressings and stampings, but is sturdy and durable. It has a conventional fixed butt and a sheet metal fore-end with ventilating slots. A folding cocking handle lies above the fore-end, on the left side of the bolt-extension tube, and a

detachable magazine protrudes beneath the receiver. The magazine-release catch lies ahead of the trigger guard bow.

The selector lever above the pistol grip is marked 'S' (safe, top), '1' (single shots, middle) and 'F' (automatic fire, bottom) on most of the guns made prior to 1975, the markings being repeated on the right side of the receiver so that an engraved line on the selector spindle could also show the fire-state. Guns made for the West Berlin police prior to the reunification of Germany were marked 'MAS' to avoid infringing agreements with the Soviet Union.

Heckler & Koch rifles made in Germany have achieved a truly worldwide distribution in addition to the countries in which they have been made under licence: Burma, Britain, Denmark (G3A5 subvariant), France, Iran (G3A6), Norway, Pakistan, Sweden and Turkey (G3A7). For a brief list, see John Walter, *Rifles of the World* (Krause Publications, second edition, 1998).

An exploded-view drawing of the 7.62mm G3A3 rifle. This is the later version, with synthetic furniture.

Automatic rifle G3 caliber 7.62 mm × 51 NATO

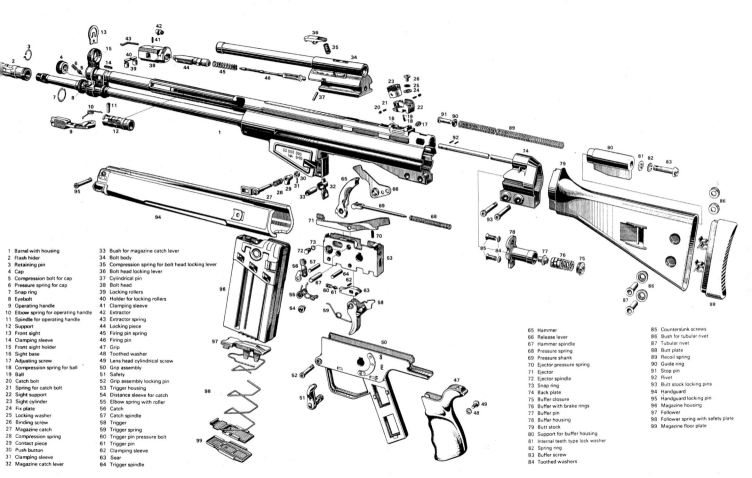

1 Barrel with housing	33 Bush for magazine catch lever	65 Hammer	85 Countersunk screws
2 Flash hider	34 Bolt body	66 Release lever	86 Bush for tubular rivet
3 Retaining pin	35 Compression spring for bolt head locking lever	67 Hammer spindle	87 Tubular rivet
4 Cap	36 Bolt head locking lever	68 Pressure spring	88 Butt plate
5 Compression bolt for cap	37 Cylindrical pin	69 Pressure shank	89 Recoil spring
6 Pressure spring for cap	38 Bolt head	70 Ejector pressure spring	90 Guide ring
7 Snap ring	39 Locking rollers	71 Ejector	91 Stop pin
8 Eyebolt	40 Holder for locking rollers	72 Ejector spindle	92 Rivet
9 Operating handle	41 Clamping sleeve	73 Snap ring	93 Butt stock locking pins
10 Elbow spring for operating handle	42 Extractor	74 Back plate	94 Handguard
11 Spindle for operating handle	43 Extractor spring	75 Buffer closure	95 Handguard locking pin
12 Support	44 Locking piece	76 Buffer with brake rings	96 Magazine housing
13 Front sight	45 Firing pin spring	77 Buffer pin	97 Follower
14 Clamping sleeve	46 Firing pin	78 Buffer housing	98 Follower spring with safety stop
15 Front sight holder	47 Grip	79 Butt stock	99 Magazine floor plate
16 Sight base	48 Toothed washer	80 Support for buffer housing	
17 Adjusting screw	49 Lens head cylindrical screw	81 Internal teeth type lock washer	
18 Compression spring for ball	50 Grip assembly	82 Spring ring	
19 Ball	51 Safety	83 Buffer screw	
20 Catch bolt	52 Grip assembly locking pin	84 Toothed washers	
21 Spring for catch bolt	53 Trigger housing		
22 Sight support	54 Distance sleeve for catch		
23 Sight cylinder	55 Elbow spring with roller		
24 Fix plate	56 Catch		
25 Locking washer	57 Catch spindle		
26 Binding screw	58 Trigger		
27 Magazine catch	59 Trigger spring		
28 Compression spring	60 Trigger pin pressure bolt		
29 Contact piece	61 Trigger pin		
30 Push button	62 Clamping sleeve		
31 Clamping sleeve	63 Sear		
32 Magazine catch lever	64 Trigger spindle		

A G3A4, with the butt retracted.

assembly. The auxiliary trigger lies on the left side of the HK79 frame above the barrel, and a ladder-pattern grenade-launching sight – subsequently replaced by a radial drum on the fore-end – is attached to the receiver top. The breech of the single-shot launcher drops open after it has been unlatched, though the striker must be cocked manually.

G3A1 Delayed by prolonged trials, this was not formally approved until October 1963. The retractable butt slid in grooves pressed into the sides of the receiver and was locked by a catch under the special receiver cap.

G3A2 This variant was approved in June 1962. The principal change seems to have been the advent of a free-floating barrel, improving accuracy. Many older guns were rebuilt to G3A2 standards during overhaul and had an additional 'FS' mark on the left side of the magazine housing beneath the original date of manufacture.

G3A3 Adopted in December 1964, this had a solid synthetic butt (cf., G3A4). Changes were made to the front sight, and the modified flash suppressor/muzzle brake handled NATO-standard grenades. A three-round burst mechanism, developed in 1968 though generally omitted from the

German service rifles, customarily occupied a fourth position on the selector. However, it could sometimes be substituted for the auto-fire option.

Changes dating from 1974 simplified the pistol grip, the fore-end and the selector lever. Additional changes were made in 1986, when synthetic butt/pistol grip sub-frames and ambidextrous safety catches were adopted. The safety mark became a white diagonal cross superimposed on a white bullet in a rectangular border; single-shot fire was indicated by a red bullet, three-shot bursts by three red bullets, and fully automatic operation by seven red bullets.

G3A4 Adopted concurrently with the G3A3, this had a retractable butt.

G3 TGS Dating from 1985, the G3 Tactical Group System (TGS) rifle has an HK79 grenade launcher instead of the standard fore-end/handguard

A Bundeswehr soldier with a G3A4 rifle, with its butt extended.

G3 INKAS Announced in 1987, this has been offered with fixed or retractable butts. The rifles have an integral infra-red laser sighting system used in conjunction with Philips *Elektro-Spezial* BM-8028 image intensifying goggles. Built into the cocking handle tube, the laser projector is activated by a switch behind the front sight.

G3 SG/1 This sniper rifle supplemented the otherwise standard G3 Zf (q.v.) in 1973. SG/1 rifles were built on actions which had shown exemplary accuracy during test-firing, and had a special set-trigger system. This could only be used with the selector lever set to 'E', whereupon the small blade protruding ahead of the pistol grip was pressed to 'set' the front trigger. The adjustable pull could be set as low as 2.75lb, compared with the standard 5.7lb. If the selector lever was moved after the mechanism had been set, but before a shot was fired, the system automatically reverted to normal operation. Most G3 SG/1 rifles had a bipod, an auxiliary cheek piece, and a Zeiss 1.5-6x optical sight.

G3 Zf Some otherwise standard rifles, selected for accuracy, have been sold as snipers' weapons (Zf, *Zielfernrohr* or telescope sight). They are uncommon.

MSG3 Built since 1988 on the basis of specially selected G3 actions restricted to semi-automatic fire, these have specially honed (but otherwise standard) triggers and bolt-closing devices to reduce cocking noise. Developed specifically for the *Bundeswehr* and German police, the *MSG3* has a standard barrel, an adjustable comb and butt plate, a fixed-leg bipod, and conventional open sights.

MSG90 A variant of the MSG3, this has a heavyweight barrel and a bipod with adjustable legs. Most guns lack the standard drum sight.

Assault rifle: Gewehr 3 (G3)
Made by Heckler & Koch GmbH & Co., Oberndorf/Neckar, Germany

Specification Standard G3A3, fixed butt
Data from manufacturer's manual,

Brief Description of the Automatic Rifle G3, August 1983 edition
Calibre 7.62mm (.300in)
Cartridge 7.62x51 NATO, rimless
Operation Delayed blowback, selective fire
Locking system Rollers on the bolt
Length 1025mm (40.68in)
Weight 4.4kg (9.68lb) without magazine
Barrel 450mm (17.71in), 4 grooves, right-hand twist
Magazine 20-round detachable box
Rate of fire 500–600rds/min
Muzzle velocity 780–800m/sec (2458–2624ft/sec) with standard SS77 ball ammunition

The G3 SG/1 had an optical sight and a special trigger system.

Developed in 1963 to capitalise on the success of the AR-15 (M16) rifle, this was essentially a G3 modified to chamber 5.56mm ammunition. The first series-made HK33 rifles dated from 1965.

HK33A2 The standard fixed-butt rifle weighed 3.6kg (7.95lb) with an empty magazine.

HK33A3 A retractable-butt variant of the HK33A2, this was mechanically identical with its prototype.

HK33 Zf Based on the HK33A2, this was a selected (but otherwise standard) rifle with an optical sight. It has been touted with limited success.

HK33KA1 Introduced in 1967, this short-barrelled gun was usually fitted with a retractable butt. A fixed butt was optional, but reduced the value of shortening the barrel.

HK33E The original HK33, successful enough to attract limited military interest, developed into the improved E pattern in 1983. By 1985, the HK33E had gained a synthetic pistol grip sub-frame. The improved ambidextrous safety catch/selector system incorporated a three-shot burst-fire mechanism.

HK33EC A2 This was a fixed-butt gun with a special forest-green camouflage finish, introduced to minimise heat absorption at high temperatures.

HK33ES A2 A version of the EC A2 pattern with a two-tone desert-sand camouflage finish.

HK33EC A3 Mechanically identical with the EC A2 gun, this was distinguished by its retractable butt.

HK33ES A3 An ES A2 with a retractable butt.

HK33KC A short barrelled version of the full-length patterns.

HK33KS Similar to the short-barrelled HK33KC, but with a retractable butt.

Typical HK33 rifles with fixed and retractable butts.

Automatic **Rifle HK 33 E** Calibre 5,56 mm x 45

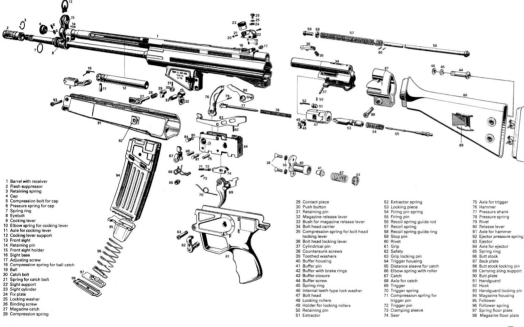

1 Barrel with receiver	29 Contact piece	52 Extractor spring	75 Axle for trigger
2 Flash suppressor	30 Push button	53 Locking piece	76 Hammer
3 Retaining spring	31 Retaining pin	54 Firing pin spring	77 Pressure shank
4 Cap	32 Magazine release lever	55 Firing pin	78 Pressure spring
5 Compression bolt for cap	33 Bush for magazine release lever	56 Recoil spring guide rod	79 Rivet
6 Pressure spring for cap	34 Bolt head carrier	57 Recoil spring	80 Release lever
7 Spring ring	35 Compression spring for bolt head	58 Recoil spring guide ring	81 Axle for hammer
8 Eyebolt	locking lever	59 Stop pin	82 Ejector pressure spring
9 Cocking lever	36 Bolt head locking lever	60 Rivet	83 Ejector
10 Elbow spring for cocking lever	37 Cylindrical pin	61 Grip	84 Axle for ejector
11 Axle for cocking lever	38 Countersunk screws	62 Safety	85 Spring ring
12 Cocking lever support	39 Toothed washers	63 Grip locking pin	86 Butt stock
13 Front sight	40 Buffer housing	64 Trigger housing	87 Back plate
14 Retaining pin	41 Buffer pin	65 Distance sleeve for catch	88 Butt stock locking pin
15 Front sight holder	42 Buffer with brake rings	66 Elbow spring with roller	89 Carrying sling support
16 Sight base	43 Buffer closure	67 Catch	90 Butt plate
17 Adjusting screw	44 Buffer screw	68 Axle for catch	91 Handguard
18 Compression spring for ball catch	45 Spring ring	69 Trigger	92 Hook
19 Ball	46 Internal teeth type lock washer	70 Trigger spring	93 Handguard locking pin
20 Catch bolt	47 Bolt head	71 Compression spring for	94 Magazine housing
21 Spring for catch bolt	48 Locking rollers	trigger pin	95 Follower
22 Sight support	49 Holder for locking rollers	72 Trigger pin	96 Follower spring
23 Sight cylinder	50 Retaining pin	73 Clamping sleeve	97 Spring floor plate
24 Fix plate	51 Extractor	74 Sear	98 Magazine floor plate
25 Locking washer			
26 Binding screw			
27 Magazine catch			
28 Compression spring			

HECKLER & KOCH GMBH HK

An exploded-view diagram of the 5.56mm HK33E rifle.

Assault rifle
Made by Heckler & Koch GmbH &
Co., Oberndorf/Neckar, Germany

Specification Standard HK33E,
  fixed butt
  Data from manufacturer's
  handbook, *Brief Description of
  the Automatic Rifle HK33E,*
  dated October 1983
Calibre 5.56mm (.223in)
Cartridge 5.56x45, rimless
Operation Delayed blowback,
  selective fire
Locking system Rollers on the
  bolt head
Length 930mm (36.22in) with butt
  extended
Weight 3.65kg (8.05lb) without
  magazine
Barrel 390mm (15.35in),
  4 grooves, right-hand twist
Magazine 25-round detachable
  box
Rate of fire about 750rds/min
Muzzle velocity 920m/sec
  (3020ft/sec) with US M193 ball
  ammunition

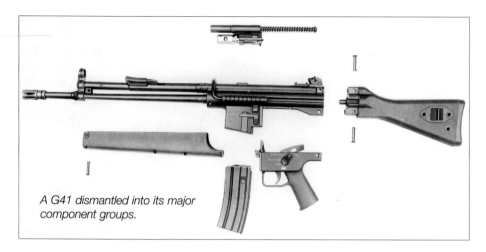

A G41 dismantled into its major component groups.

Introduced in 1983 to replace the HK33, this incorporated a mechanical hold-open and a bolt-closing device on the right side of the action inspired by the M16A1. The ejection port was fitted with a hinged cover, the magazine attachment and optical-sight mounts were altered to conform with NATO standards, and tritium sight inserts were fitted. The guns were designed for a minimum life of 20,000 rounds, the barrels being rifled for US M193 ball ammunition, making a turn in 178mm (7in).

New synthetic butt/pistol grip sub-frames were adopted in 1986, together with an ambidextrous safety catch. The safety mark became a white diagonal cross superimposed on a white bullet; single-shot fire was indicated by a red bullet, three-shot bursts by three red bullets, and fully automatic operation by seven red bullets.

G41A1 This was a variant of the standard G41, with rifling making a turn in 305mm (12in). This suited it to Belgian SS109 ball ammunition.

G41A2 A retractable-butt gun rifled for M193 ammunition (one turn in 178mm).

G41A3 Another retractable-butt variant, rifled for the SS109 ball cartridge.

G41K This was a short-barrel derivative, overall length being about 13cm (5.1in) less than normal.

G41 TGS Announced in 1985, this had a 40mm HK79 grenade launcher beneath the fore-end. The oldest guns had a ladder-pattern auxiliary sight on top of the receiver, in front of the standard drum, but this was soon replaced by a radial sight on the right side of the fore-end. The G41K TGS was a short-barrelled derivative.

G41 INKAS Similar to the G3 variant (q.v.), found with fixed or retractable butts, this rifle had an integral infra-red laser projector in the cocking-handle tube. The projector was used in conjunction with Philips *Elektro-Spezial* BM 8028 goggles. G41K INKAS was a short-barrelled version.

GR3 Adapted from the HK33/G41 in the mid-1980s and introduced in 1988, this gun had a simple 1.5x optical sight – adjustable for elevation and windage – on a permanent receiver-top mount.

A G41 TGS, with single-shot 40mm grenade launcher and a ladder-type grenade-launching sight on top of the receiver.

Assault rifle: Gewehr 41
Made by Heckler & Koch GmbH & Co., Oberndorf/Neckar, Germany

Specification Standard G41, fixed butt
Data from the manufacturer's handbook, *Brief Description of the G41*, dating from May 1985
Calibre 5.56mm (.223in)
Cartridge 5.56x45, rimless
Operation Delayed blowback, selective fire
Locking system Rollers on the bolt head
Length 997mm (39.25in)
Weight 4.1kg (9.04lb) without magazine
Barrel 450mm (17.7in), 4 grooves, right-hand twist
Magazine 20- or 30-round detachable box
Rate of fire *c.* 850rds/min
Muzzle velocity Not specified (*see* HK33)

Dimensions paralleled their HK33 equivalents, though GR3 patterns were all about 285g (10oz) heavier.

GR3C A2 The basic fixed-butt rifle had forest-green camouflage on the receiver and fore-end.

GR3S A2 Mechanically identical with the GR3C version, this was distinguished by its desert-sand camouflage finish.

GR3C A3 Similar to the A2 pattern, this had a retractable butt and forest-green finish.

GR3S A3 A variant combining a retractable butt and desert-sand camouflage.

GR3KC A straightforward amalgamation of a short barrel, a retractable stock, and forest-green camouflage.

GR3KS Identical with the GR3KC pattern in all respects except colouring, this had desert-sand camouflage.

The optically sighted version of the G41, the G41 Zf, has been made only in small numbers.

The PSG-1, a specialist sniping rifle, is a sophisticated semi-automatic variant of the G3.

Introduced in 1982, this G3 derivative had a butt with a detachable saddle-type cheek piece (similar to those found on H&K light machine-guns) and a shoulder-plate adjustable for length and rake. The separate anatomical walnut pistol grip had an adjustable palm rest. A special heavyweight barrel was used, though the standard G3 action was limited to semi-automatic fire; special attention to the trigger gave a smooth 3.3lb pull.

Mounted and adjusted as an integral part of the weapon, the 6x42 optical sight had an illuminated range-finding reticle graduated for 100–600m.

Semi-automatic sniper rifle: Präzisions-Scharfschützengewehr 1, PSG-1
Made by Heckler & Koch GmbH & Co., Oberndorf/Neckar, Germany

Specification Standard pattern
  Data from the manufacturer's handbook, *Brief Description of the High-Precision Marksman's Rifle PSG-1*, dated May 1983
Calibre 7.62mm (.300in)
Cartridge 7.62x51 NATO, rimless
Operation Delayed blowback, single shots only
Locking system Rollers on the bolt head
Length 1208mm (47.56in*)

Weight 8.1kg (17.86lb*) without magazine; a loaded 5-round magazine weighs 100g (3.5oz*), and a tripod weighs 1025g (2.26lb*)
Barrel 650mm (25.59in*), 4 grooves, right-hand twist
Magazine 5- or 10-round detachable box
Rate of fire NA
Muzzle velocity Not specified

The PSG-1 dismantled into its major component groups.

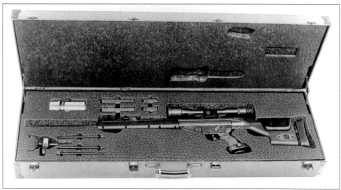

The PSG-1 in its foam-lined case.

Heckler & Koch G36   Germany

The 5.56mm Heckler & Koch G36E, an export version of the latest German service rifle, has an optical sight in the carrying handle.

The first Heckler & Koch rifle to abandon the delayed blowback roller-lock system, excepting the caseless-cartridge G11, this was adopted by the *Bundeswehr* in 1995 to avert a financial crisis that had caused the planned re-equipment with the G11K3 to cease after only 1000 had been made for extended field trials. The gas-operated G36 is much more conventional that the revolutionary gun it replaced, with a rotating bolt, six-groove concentric rifling, and a 3x optical sight set into the carrying handle. Most guns also have a red-dot collimating sight above the optical unit, facilitating snap shooting. The skeletal butt can be folded to reduce overall dimensions, in common with most modern rifles, but the slab-sided appearance of the gun is distinctive.

G36K Issued to German Special Forces and some Federal police units, this is simply a short-barrelled version of the standard rifle. Overall length is merely 858mm (33.78in) with the butt extended, or 613mm (24.13in) with the butt retracted.

G36E An export-only version of the G36 with a 1.5x optical sight. The G36KE is identical, but has the shorter barrel.

Assault rifle
Made by Heckler & Koch GmbH & Co., Oberndorf/Neckar, Germany

Specification Standard infantry pattern
  Data from Ian Hogg, *The Greenhill Military Small Arms Data Book* (1999)
Calibre 5.56mm (.223in)
Cartridge 5.56x45, rimless
Operation Gas operated, selective fire
Locking system Rotating bolt
Length 998mm (39.29in), butt extended; 758mm (29.84in), butt retracted
Weight 3.43kg (7.56lb*)
Barrel 480mm (18.90in), 6 grooves, right-hand twist
Magazine 30-round detachable box
Rate of fire 750rds/min
Muzzle velocity 920m/sec (3018ft/sec) with SS109 ball ammunition

Mauser 66 SP

Designed by Walter Gehmann of Karlsruhe in the early 1960s, this unique short-action rifle presents a complete departure from traditional Mausers. The prototype was exhibited at the international arms fair (IWA) in Nürnberg in 1965, and series-made sporting guns appeared in 1966.

The reduction in length is due largely to the location of the magazine between the trigger and the bolt, and by telescoping the bolt and bolt carrier. As the bolt is retracted to open the breech, the handle strikes the bolt-carrier bridge; bolt and carrier then run back together over the wrist of the stock. The ejector and extractor are both carried in the bolt head; a safety catch lies on the right side of the cocking-piece shroud; and the bolt stop protrudes from the right side of the stock above the trigger.

Cap-head bolts retaining the receiver ring and the backsight block can be loosened, allowing the barrel/receiver ring assembly to be replaced after the bolt has been opened. Shutting the action automatically indexes the barrel, the retaining bolts are replaced and the gun is ready for use.

The sniper rifle appeared in 1976, chambered only for the .308 Winchester/7.62x51mm NATO cartridge. Specially selected for accuracy, the action is fitted to a heavy barrel with an efficient flash-hider/muzzle brake. The massive wood stock has a thumbhole grip, an adjustable cheek piece, and a butt which can be lengthened with spacers. Zeiss Diavari 1.5-6x42 optical sights are usually fitted.

The 66 SP offers advantages over most conventional bolt-action patterns, as it has an ultra-fast lock time and – owing to the position of the handle – the bolt can be operated with minimal disturbance of aim. It has been used in small numbers by military, paramilitary and police throughout the world, but the restricted magazine capacity is generally regarded as disadvantageous.

Bolt-action sniper rifle
Made by Mauser-Werke Oberndorf GmbH, Oberndorf/Neckar

Specification
Data from a manufacturer's advertising leaflet, *Scharfschützengewehr Sniper-Rifle Mod. 66 SP,* dated March 1986
Calibre 7.62mm (.300in)
Cartridge 7.62x51 NATO, rimless
Operation Manual, single shot only
Locking system Rotating bolt
Length 1140mm (44.88in*)
Weight 5.5kg (12.13lb*) without optical sight
Barrel 650mm (25.59in*) without muzzle brake, 4 grooves, right-hand twist
Magazine 3-round internal box
Rate of fire NA
Muzzle velocity Not given (*c.* 860m/sec [2822ft/sec] with SS77 ball ammunition)

Distinguished by its ultra-short action, the Mauser 66 SP has sold in small numbers to military, police and counter-terrorist forces across the world.

Mauser 86 SR   Germany

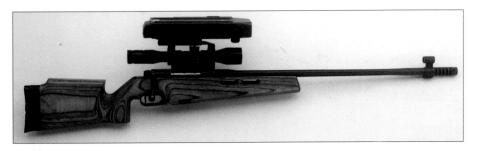

The Mauser Model 86, seen here with a laser rangefinder above the optical sight, has a conventional bolt action. A few guns have been sold as snipers' weapons.

Developed from the Model 77 and Model 83 sporting/target rifles, originally introduced in 1978, this was chambered only for the .308 Winchester round (7.62x51 NATO). It retained the basic shape of the Model 83; however, the Model 86 bolt had lugs locking into the receiver ring instead of the bridge in a search for better accuracy. The sight rail above the breech was lowered and a laminated stock was used. Fluted to save weight while retaining rigidity, the barrel had an efficient flash suppressor/muzzle brake. Nine-cartridge magazines were standard. A synthetic/thumbhole-type stock option was announced in 1989.

SR 93 This is a greatly simplified form of the Model 86 with a bolt handle that can be instantly changed from the right to left side of the breech. The synthetic stock is bolted to an alloy chassis – an idea clearly inspired by British Accuracy International designs – and the barrel is allowed to float freely in a search for accuracy. Chambered only for the powerful .300 Winchester or .338 Lapua Magnum cartridges, the SR 93 does not seem to have been as successful as its promoters expected; the *Bundeswehr* remains wedded to the Heckler & Koch PSG-1, and is said to actively considering the British AI AW rifle.

Bolt-action sniper rifle:
Scharfschützengewehr 86 (SG 86 or SR 86)
Made by Mauser-Werke Oberndorf GmbH, Oberndorf/Neckar, 1987 to date

Specification Standard version
 Data from a manufacturer's advertising leaflet, *Scharfschützengewehr Modell 86 SR/Sniper-Rifle Model 86 SR,* dated December 1989

Calibre 7.62mm (.300in)
Cartridge 7.62x51 NATO, rimless
Operation Manual, single shots only
Locking system Rotating bolt
Length 1194–1210mm
 (47.01–47.64in*), depending on butt-plate adjustment
Weight 4.90kg (10.56lb*) without optical sight
Barrel 650mm (25.59in*) without muzzle brake, 4 grooves, right-hand twist
Magazine 9-round detachable box
Rate of fire NA
Muzzle velocity Not given
 (*c.* 860m/sec [2822ft/sec] with SS77 ball ammunition)

Galil

Israel

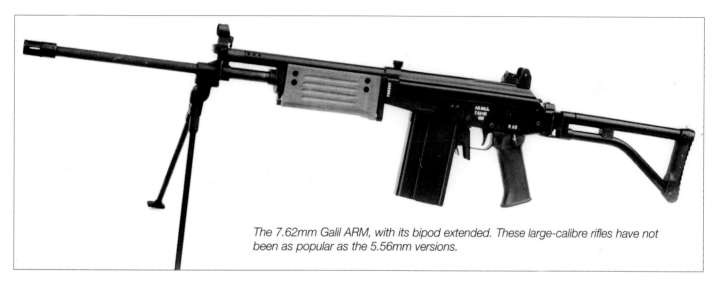

The 7.62mm Galil ARM, with its bipod extended. These large-calibre rifles have not been as popular as the 5.56mm versions.

The Israeli Army acquired the first of many FAL rifles in the early 1960s, the guns remaining regulation issue until the advent of the 5.56mm M16A1 and Galil rifles. The earliest weapons were purchased directly from Fabrique Nationale, but later examples were assembled by Israeli Military Industries. These had FN-made receivers, but the remaining components were made locally.

Guns assembled by IMI exhibited changes suggested by combat in desert conditions: the butt had a lower comb; the fore-end was pressed-metal, with a short finely fluted wooden grip; the cocking handle was modified to double as a bolt-closing device; the front-sight/gas-plug assembly was improved; and the dismantling catch was recessed to reduce the chances of accidentally opening the receiver. However, the

Israeli authorities were never satisfied with the FAL and, impressed by the performance of AKM rifles in the Six-Day War of 1967, decided to produce a modified Kalashnikov. Known as the Galil, in honour of the engineer responsible for the transformation, the Israeli rifle approximates to the Finnish m/62 – indeed, the earliest guns were apparently built on Valmet-made receivers. The basic Kalashnikov action, improved in detail, was amalgamated with a simple gas system lacking a regulator.

AR Offered in 5.56mm or 7.62mm, this was a long-barrelled ARM without the bipod and cocking handle. It also had a simplified synthetic fore-end.

ARM Introduced in 1971, this had a tubular plastic pistol grip, a tubular skeletal butt folding to the right, and a radial selector, marked 'S', 'A' and 'R', that closed the ejection port in its uppermost (safe) position. The cocking handle was bent upward so that the rifle could be cocked with either hand, and a folding carrying handle lay above the chamber. The earliest rifles had fluted wooden fore-ends, but later examples usually had synthetic furniture; 7.62mm examples were noticeably bigger than the 5.56mm pattern.

The bipod of the standard ARM pivoted on the gas block to double as a wire cutter. A short flash suppressor/compensator was fitted to the muzzle and a short US-type bayonet could be attached. Among the most obvious

The 5.56mm Galil SAR.

features of the Galil was the backsight at the rear of the breech cover, accompanied by projecting ears and a folding 100m night sight with luminescent tritium dots.

Export patterns were generally marked in English; Israeli Defence Force rifles, stamped in Hebrew, also displayed a sword and olive branch

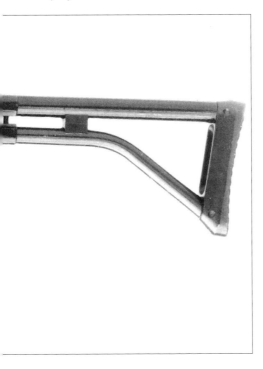

inside a six-point star on the left side of the receiver above the pistol grip. Many guns made after about 1980 may bear the Israeli Military Industries trademark of a sword and an olive branch superimposed on a cogwheel.

MAR (Marksman's Assault Rifle)
Introduced in 1996, this is little more than a specially selected 5.56mm ARM rifled for the US M193 bullet (one turn in 178mm [7in]). The butt has an adjustable cheek piece, a bracket for an optical sight is anchored to the left side of the receiver above the magazine, and a special adjustable-leg bipod is attached beneath the fore-end. The gun weighs about 4.95kg (10.88lb) with sights, bipod and an empty magazine.

SAR This was a short-barrel variant of the AR, folding to just 615mm (24.2in).

Sniper Developed for Israeli Army snipers in the early 1980s, this special semi-automatic 7.62mm AR-type Galil had a heavyweight barrel, a large tubular muzzle brake/compensator, and a two-stage trigger. The bipod was moved back to pivot on the receiver instead of the gas block, relieving the barrel of unnecessary stress. The folding wooden butt had a cheek piece and a ventilated rubber recoil pad. The guns were about 1115mm (43.9in) long and weighed 6.4kg (14.1lb) with the

bipod. A standard two-position aperture backsight was fitted to the receiver, but a bracket attached to the left side of the receiver accepted a 6x40 Nimrod telescope or any NATO-standard infra-red and image-intensifying night-vision sight.

Assault rifle
Made by Israeli Military Industries, Ramat ha-Sharon

Specification Standard ARM infantry rifle
  Data from manufacturer's advertising leaflet, Galil 7.62mm Assault Rifle, dated January 1982

Calibre 7.62mm (.223in)
Cartridge 7.62x51 NATO, rimless
Operation Gas operated, selective fire
Locking system Rotating bolt
Length 1050mm (41.34in*) with butt extended; 810mm (31.89in*) with butt folded
Weight 4.3kg (9.48lb*) with bipod and carrying handle, but without magazine; loaded 25-round magazine, 900g (1.98lb*)
Barrel 535mm (21.06in*), 4 grooves, right-hand twist
Magazine 25-round detachable box
Rate of fire 650rds/min
Muzzle velocity 850m/sec (2789ft/sec*) with S77 ball ammunition

Beretta BM59 Italy

The first BM59, dating from 1958, were simply shortened selective-fire 7.62x51 M1 Garands (q.v.) with detachable box magazines. Many guns of this type have been supplied to Indonesia and Nigeria, whilst smaller quantities were distributed throughout the world.

BM59D Introduced in 1959, this was a variant of the standard BM59 with an auxiliary pistol grip behind the trigger.

BM59R A 1959-vintage derivation of the BM59 with a rate-reducing device built into the trigger mechanism.

BM59GL Dating from 1959–60, this minor variant was distinguished by a grenade launcher fitted to the muzzle.

BM59 Mk I This had an improved trigger system and a 'tri-compensator' – a muzzle fitting serving as a muzzle brake, flash suppressor and compensator, but also capable of accepting a US-style M1 bayonet and Mecar rifle grenades.

BM59 Mk II Essentially similar to the Mk I, this had an additional pistol grip behind the trigger guard to aid control when firing automatically. It was also fitted with a winter trigger, a bipod attached to the gas tube, and a shoulder strap on the butt plate.

BM59 Mk III This rifle lacked the bipod, but offered an auxiliary pistol grip ahead of the magazine and a folding steel stock strong enough to withstand grenade launching.

BM59 Mk IV Intended as a light support weapon, this had a heavy barrel and a stock not unlike that of the later US M14A1 (q.v.).

BM60CB Introduced in 1960, this could fire three-round bursts instead of fully automatically.

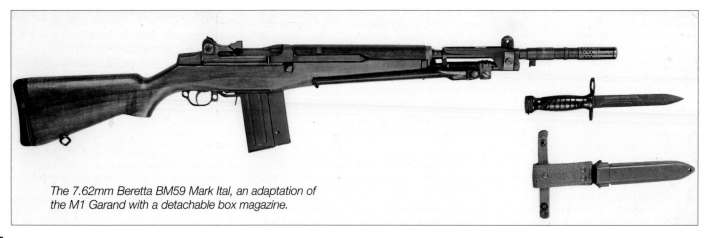

The 7.62mm Beretta BM59 Mark Ital, an adaptation of the M1 Garand with a detachable box magazine.

The BM59 Ital *Alpini was intended for mountain troops. Note the folding butt, the separate pistol grip, and the compensator/grenade-launcher tube.*

BM59 Mk Ital After extensive trials, the Italian Army adopted this variant in 1962. The service rifle had a conventional pistol-gripped wood stock, a bipod around the gas tube, and a grenade-launcher sight folding down behind the front-sight block.

BM59 Ital *Tipo Alpini* Intended to arm mountain troops, this had a folding butt and a pistol grip behind the trigger.

BM59 Ital *Tipo Paracudisti* This paratroop rifle was similar to the *Alpini* version, but had a detachable compensator.

BM59 Ital A This was simply a standard Ital with a folding butt.

BM59SL Restricted to semi-automatic fire, this was an adapted M1 Garand with a detachable box magazine.

Auto-loading rifle: Fucile automatico Beretta, Mo. 1959
Made by Armi Pietro Beretta SpA, Rome

Specification BM59 Ital *Tipo Paracudisti*
Data from the manufacturer's handbook, *Beretta 7.62mm NATO BM59,* dated July 1966
Calibre 7.62mm (.300in)
Cartridge 7.62x51mm, rimless
Operation Gas operated, selective fire

Locking system Rotating bolt
Length 1225mm (48.22in), butt extended
Weight 4.56kg (10.06lb) without accessories; 5.775kg (12.74lb) with loaded magazine, bayonet and sling
Barrel 467.7mm (18.41in) without grenade launcher/compensator, 4 grooves, right-hand twist
Magazine 20-round detachable box
Rate of fire 810rds/min
Muzzle velocity 810m/sec (2657ft/sec*) with NATO SS77 ball ammunition

The original 5.56mm Beretta AR70, with optical sight and bipod.

Announced in 1970 after a lengthy development programme dating back to 1965, this presented a conventional appearance even though its receiver was made largely of pressings. The earliest AR70 had a ribbed synthetic fore-end. The pistol grip was originally chequered wood, but was soon changed to a synthetic pattern matching the fore-end.

The rotary selector lay above the pistol grip on the left side of the receiver (up for automatic fire, back for single shots, down to lock the trigger), the cocking handle was on the right, and conventional sights were accompanied by folding grenade-launching patterns.

AR70 rifles accepted optical or image-intensifying sights, and could fire grenades from a NATO-standard launcher. A bipod and carrying handle transformed them into light support weapons, and an American-style knife bayonet was available if required.

By 1983, substantial quantities of Beretta rifles had been purchased by the Italian air force and special counter-terrorist units such as the *Nuclei Operativi Centrali di Sicurezza* and the *Gruppi per Interventi Speciali*. Compared with the earliest examples, the perfected derivatives of the AR70 offered a great many detail improvements. In particular, the folding stock was strengthened and the original ribbed handguard gave way to a fluted pattern with ventilation slots. However, field trials and active paramilitary service showed that improvements could still be made and the AR70/90 was substituted.

SC70 A folding-butt derivative of the AR70, comparable in size and capable of accepting the same range of auxiliary sights.

SC70 *versione corta* This ultra-short

A later version of the Beretta AR70, dating from 1983. Note the extensive changes in construction compared with the earlier gun.

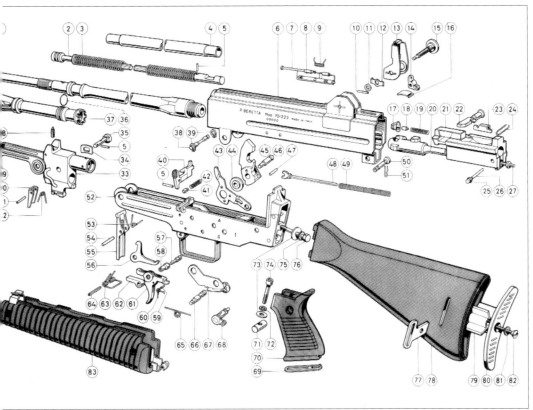

An exploded-view drawing of the Beretta AR-70.

version of the SC70 appeared in 1974. It was 820mm (32.28in) overall with the stock extended – 598mm (23.54in) when folded – and lacked both the grenade-launching sights and the muzzle sleeve.

Assault rifle: Fucile d'Assalto AR70 Made by Pietro Beretta SpA, Gardone Val Trompia (Brescia), 1970–83

Specification AR70, fixed butt
  Data from manufacturer's handbook, *Beretta mod. 70/.223 weapons system,* undated (*c.* 1975)
Calibre 5.56mm (.223in)
Cartridge 5.56x45, rimless
Operation Gas operated, selective fire
Locking system Rotating bolt
Length 955mm (37.6in*)
Weight 3.5kg (7.7lb*) without magazine or sling; loaded 30-round magazine, 600g (1.315lb*); bayonet 283g (10oz*)
Barrel 450mm (17.8in*) without grenade launcher, 4 or 6 grooves, right-hand twist
Magazine 30-round detachable box
Rate of fire *c.* 700rds/min
Muzzle velocity 960m/sec (3150ft/sec*) with US M193 ball ammunition

Beretta AR70/90 Italy

A typical Beretta AR70/90, dating from the late 1980s. A channel is cut through the carrying handle to allow the sights to be used.

Rigorous service trials revealed minor flaws in the AR70 and an accompanying light machine-gun, and work began in 1984 to revise the design. The first 70/90 rifle appeared in 1985. Eventually, after protracted testing, the perfected version was selected in July 1990 to replace the BM59 in Italian service, and the first large-scale deliveries occurred in 1992.

The major change is internal. The bolt of the AR70 had reciprocated on rails pressed into the receiver, but this method did not satisfy the army and so hardened steel rails have been inserted in the AR70/90 frame.

The new straight-line layout results from raising the heel of the butt, and a detachable carrying handle now lies on the top of the receiver. An ambidextrous selector/safety catch unit is fitted, while changes have been made to the receiver and pistol grip. Bipods can be removed at will.

SC70/90 This is the standard folding-butt version of the AR70/90, though the two patterns are otherwise mechanically identical.

SCS70/90 A short-barrelled version of the SC70/90, this lacks the grenade-launching tube on the muzzle.

SCP70/90 Intended for paratroop use *(Tipo Paracudisti)*, this short-barrelled gun has a folding stock, a grenade launcher on the muzzle, and an auxiliary folding sight on the gas-port block.

Assault rifle: Fucile d'Assalto AR70/90
Made by P. Beretta SpA, Gardone Val Trompia (Brescia), 1985 to date

Specification 1988 pattern
  Data from Ian Hogg, *The Greenhill Military Small Arms Data Book* (1999)
Calibre 5.56mm (.223in)
Cartridge 5.56x45mm, rimless.
Operation Gas operated, automatic fire only
Locking system Rotating bolt
Length 995mm (39.17in*)
Weight 3.94kg (8.69lb*) without magazine
Barrel 450mm (17.72in*), 6 grooves, right-hand twist
Magazine 30-round detachable box
Rate of fire 600–650rds/min
Muzzle velocity 930m/sec (3051ft/sec*) with US M193 ball ammunition

The Beretta SCP70/90 of 1992 is intended for paratroops. Note the optional grenade launcher/compensator, with a lug for an American-type knife bayonet.

92

Beretta Sniper Italy

Introduced commercially in 1984 in three action lengths, Beretta's bolt-action sporting rifle is basically a Mauser. The extractor is a small claw let into the side of the bolt head; the plunger-type ejector is mounted in the recessed bolt face. The Model 500 Sniper (1985) has been offered only in 7.62x51 NATO, with a heavy barrel, a conical muzzle brake/flash suppressor, and an adjustable bipod attached to a bar projecting from the fore-end. A detachable box magazine can be obtained, and the special thumbhole stock has a removable cheek piece/comb unit.

Bolt-action sniper rifle
Made by Pietro Beretta SpA, Gardone Val Trompia, 1984 to date

Specification Standard gun
   Data from manufacturer's advertising
   literature, undated (*c.* 1987)
Calibre 7.62mm (.30in)
Cartridge 7.62x51 NATO, rimless

Operation Manual, single shots only
Locking system Rotating bolt
Length 1165mm (45.87in*)
Weight 5.55kg (12.24lb*) with empty
   magazine; bipod, 950g (2.09lb*)
Barrel 586mm (23.07in*), 4 grooves,
   right-hand twist
Magazine 5-round detachable box
Rate of fire NA
Muzzle velocity Not specified

A Beretta Model 500 Sniper rifle. The design of the thumbhole butt is unmistakable.

Type 64   Japan

A search to find an auto-loader for the Japanese forces began in earnest in 1958, when a team of military personnel and Howa civilian technicians under the leadership of General Koni Iwashita began test-firing in April. Experiments continued until the Howa-pattern R-6 appeared, progressing through several stages until the R-6E (Modified) was approved for production.

Adopted in April 1964, the Type 64 is characterised by attention to detail to reduce length and weight to suit the stature of the average Japanese soldier. Special reduced-charge 7.62mm cartridges are standard, though conventional full-power ammunition can be used if the gas regulator has been adjusted accordingly. A short-stroke piston system allows a distinctive straight-line layout, and the trigger mechanism incorporates an unusual linear hammer running back into the butt housing. The handguard is a ventilated metal pressing, a bipod can be obtained, and a shoulder strap folds on the butt plate. Production ceased in 1985, pending the investigation of 5.56mm designs.

Type 89 This lightweight adaptation of the Type 64, now the service rifle of the Japanese Defence Force, has a rotating bolt and a 'soft action' operating system that allows the propellant gas tapped from the bore time to expand before reaching the piston head. Another idiosyncrasy is evident in the trigger system, where the burst-firing components are isolated from the single-shot/automatic functions so that the gun will still fire if the burst-unit fails in combat. The fixed-butt Type 89 is 916mm (36.07in) long and weighs about 3.5kg (7.69lb) without its magazine, but a folding-butt variant has also been made.

Automatic rifle: 64-shiki jidoju
Made by Howa Machinery Company, Nagoya, 1965–85

Specification Standard version
  Data from Ian Hogg, *The Greenhill Military Small Arms Data Book* (1999)
Calibre 7.62mm (.300in)
Cartridge 7.62x51 NATO, rimless
Operation Gas operated, selective fire
Locking system Tilting bolt
Length 989mm* (38.95in)
Weight 4.41kg* (9.72lb) with loaded magazine and bipod
Barrel 450mm (17.7in), 4 grooves, right-hand twist
Magazine 20-round detachable box
Rate of fire 475–525rds/min
Muzzle velocity 700m/sec* (2295ft/sec) with Type 64 ball ammunition

The 7.62mm Type 64 rifle.

The 5.56mm Daewoo K2 assault rifle.

A licensed copy of the M16A1 (Colt Model 603-K) has been built in what was once the government-owned Pusan arsenal, after the US Military Aid Program had provided nearly 27,000 M16A1 rifles from US Army stores. The indigenous rifles bore 'MADE IN KOREA' above an acknowledgement of the licence on the right side of the magazine, the designation and K-prefix serial number appearing on the left. Production is said to have approached 600,000 before work finished *c.* 1985. The selector was marked in Korean.

In 1983, the Pusan facilities were sold to Daewoo Precision Industries and development of new weapons began immediately, seeking to free Korea from dependence on US small arms. The prototype rifles appeared in 1984, series production beginning a year later.

The K1 carbine of 1985, equivalent to the US Army XM177E2 (*see* ArmaLite), combines the direct-impingement gas system of the M16 with the bolt carrier and twin recoil-guide rod assembly of the AR-18. The lower part of the hinged receiver resembles the M16A1, though the upper section differs greatly; the integral carrying handle has been replaced by a prominent sight protector and the butt has substantially more drop at the wrist. The K1 can fire single shots, three-round bursts or fully automatically; selectors display markings in Korean or English.

K1A1 This carbine has a longer barrel than the K1, to minimise muzzle flash, but shares the construction of its predecessors and has also been offered in semi-automatic Law Enforcement form.

K2 A rifle sharing the basic construction of the K1 carbine, this has a full-length barrel and a solid polyamide butt swinging to the right instead of a retractable pattern. The gas system has become a long-stroke piston adapted from the Soviet Kalashnikov, and the muzzle brake/compensator can accept standard rifle grenades. The K2 is 988mm (38.9in) long, weighs 3.35kg (7.38lb) without its magazine, and has an 465mm (18.3in) barrel.

Compact assault rifle
Made by Daewoo Precision Industries, Pusan

Specification K1 Carbine
   Data from John Walter, *Rifles of the World* (second edition, 1998)
Calibre 5.56mm (.223in)
Cartridge 5.56x45, rimless
Operation Gas operated, selective fire
Locking system Rotating bolt
Length 785mm* (30.9in) with stock extended
Weight 2.85kg* (6.28lb) empty
Barrel 263mm* (10.35in), 4 grooves, right-hand twist
Magazine 30-round detachable box
Rate of fire Not known
Muzzle velocity 954m/sec* (3130 ft/sec) with standard M193 bullet

The NM149MS sniper rifle, built on a reconditioned Mauser action.

Many ex-German Kar 98k rifles were issued to the Norwegian Army after the end of the Second World War, offsetting a shortage of Krags. Some guns were converted in the late 1940s for the US .30-06 (7.62x63) round, apparently for issue to the home guard, and many others were altered in the late 1950s to chamber the 7.62x51 rimless cartridge; rifles of this type are usually marked 'HÆR' (army) on the left side of the chamber.

Specially selected actions were used as the basis for .30-06 Model 59 target rifles issued to the army, given to the national shooting association, or sold commercially. The first of these had a floating barrel in a special half-stock, with a new handguard (held by a single band) and a near-vertical pistol grip. A special aperture backsight, developed

by Kongsberg in collusion with the Norma ammunition factory, was fitted on the receiver bridge. The bolt handle was customarily turned downward.

The Model 59F1 was a 7.62mm variant of the .30-06 M59, introduced in 1964 after the adoption of the Heckler & Koch G3 automatic rifle. Army sniping rifles were issued with a 4x Hertel & Reuss telescope sight in a bracket-type mount on the left side of the receiver. The most recent of these Mauser adaptations is the NM149MS sniper rifle, adopted by the army and police in 1988. A new heavyweight cold-forged barrel is fitted to a refurbished action, and a stiffening bar, which doubles as a rail for a Schmidt & Bender 6x42 sight, is fitted over the magazine aperture. Alternatively, an aperture sight can be substituted for use in conjunction with a

conventional blade-type front sight.

The beech stock is a resin-impregnated laminate, with an optional adjustable comb. The trigger is an adjustable match-quality design, and a detachable box magazine replaces the traditional internal Mauser pattern; the sight-rail, though it does not interfere with ejection, prevents the magazine being loaded through the top of the open action.

Bolt-action sniper rifle
Made by Våpensmia A/S, Dokka

Specification
Data from Ian Hogg, *The Greenhill Military Small Arms Data Book* (1999)
Calibre 7.62mm (.300in)
Cartridge 7.62x51 NATO, rimless
Operation Manual, single shots only
Locking system Rotating bolt
Length 1120mm (44.10in)
Weight 5.6kg (12.35lb*) with sights
Barrel 600mm (23.62in), 4 grooves, right-hand twist
Magazine 5-round detachable box
Rate of fire NA
Muzzle velocity about 860m/sec (2820ft/sec) with SS77 ball ammunition

AN-94　　　　　　　　　　　　　　　　　　　　　　**Russia**

Developed in the late 1980s, this rifle was first noticed in the West in 1992, when it was mistakenly identified as the Abakan (the code name applied to the Russian military assault-rifle trials). Details are still sketchy, owing to a cloak of secrecy which shrouds the project, but the AN-94 is claimed to use 'indirect [or shifted pulse] impulse' to achieve twice the efficiency of the AK-74 and 50 per cent greater efficiency than the M16. The original rifles were tested with 30- or 60-round magazines, but the latter predictably proved to be too clumsy. The butt was angular and the fore-end had a projection on the underside to prevent the support hand sliding back during automatic fire. The developed versions have a light L-shaped folding butt, a ribbed plastic fore-end with ventilating slots, and a prominent bulbous fore-end/compensator. The gas tube lies beneath the barrel.

The selector lever has been moved to the left side of the receiver above the pistol grip, where it can be activated with the thumb of the trigger hand; in addition to the locked or safe position, it can be set to give single shots, a two-round burst or automatic fire.

One of the oddest features of the Nikonov design is its ability to fire the first two shots (three in the prototypes) at a prodigious rate of 1800–2000rpm, though a cable and cog system then drops the cyclic rate to 600rpm. The secret of this performance may lie in a loading tray holding a second round ready to be rammed into the breech after the first or chambered round has been fired, but details are lacking.

The AN-94 has an external affinity with the Kalashnikov. However, the breech cover is more angular, the pistol grip lies farther back, the muzzle fittings are unmistakable, the backsight lies at the rear of the breech cover, and a bracket for optical/electro-optical sights is attached to the left side of the receiver.

Assault rifle: Avtomat Nikonova obr. 94, AN-94
Apparently made by the Izhevsk ordnance factory

Specification Standard version
　Data from John Walter, *Rifles of the World* (second edition, 1998)
Calibre 5.45mm (0.215in)
Cartridge 5.45x39 M74, rimless
Operation Gas-delayed blowback
Locking system Not known
Length 944mm* (37.15in)
Weight 3.92kg* (8.64lb) without magazine
Barrel 419mm* (16.5in?), 4 grooves, right-hand twist
Magazine 30-round detachable box
Rate of fire 1800/600rds/min
Muzzle velocity Not specified

The AN-94 rifle, still little known in the West.

CIS SAR80 Singapore

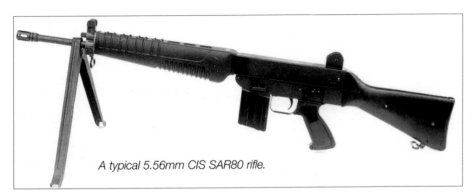

A typical 5.56mm CIS SAR80 rifle.

The fore-end was a tapering synthetic design, with vertical ribs behind the front sight. M16 magazines was standardised, together with an American-type muzzle brake/grenade launcher; bipods and a folding butt were optional.

Assault rifle
Made by Chartered Industries of Singapore Ltd, later Chartered Firearms Industries Pty Ltd, Singapore

Singapore ordered 18,000 standard and 2300 heavy-barrel CAR-15 rifles from Colt in 1966, but only about 3000 had been delivered when, in February 1967, the authorities obtained a licence to make 150,000 rifles. Production was entrusted to Chartered Industries Ltd (CIS), with technical assistance from Colt.

The first guns were made in 1970, work continuing for about a decade; about 185,000 were made. Singapore-made rifles bore the CIS trademark on the left side of the magazine housing, above an acknowledgement of the licensing agreement. Making ArmaLites involved the payment of licensing fees and when work on the M16 came to an

end, therefore, CIS produced the SA-80 – an adaptation of the ArmaLite AR-18 by way of the abortive Sterling Light Automatic Rifle.

The first prototypes appeared in 1978, most of the design studies being undertaken in England by the Sterling Engineering Co. Ltd, work being credited to Frank Waters and L. James Sullivan. Series production began in Singapore in 1981.

The SAR80 relies heavily on stampings and sheet-metal fabrication, reducing costs substantially compared with the M16. It is locked by a rotating Stoner-pattern bolt, and could be identified by crackle finish on the receiver.

Specification Standard infantry pattern
   Data from Ian Hogg, *The Greenhill
   Military Small Arms Data Book* (1999)
Calibre 5.56mm (.223in)
Cartridge 5.56x45, rimless
Operation Gas operated, selective fire
Locking system Rotating bolt
Length 970mm (38.18in)
Weight 3.70kg (8.19lb*) with empty
   magazine
Barrel 459mm (18.07in), 6 grooves,
   right-hand twist
Magazine 20- or 30-round detachable box
Rate of fire 600rds/min
Muzzle velocity 970m/sec (3182ft/sec)
   with standard ball ammunition

CIS SR88, SR88A   Singapore

*The 5.56mm SR88 assault rifle was
an improved form of the SAR80.*

This 1988-vintage improved version of the SA-80 had a slotted handguard to improve barrel ventilation, a folding carrying handle, and a new adjustable aperture pattern backsight. The US M203 grenade launcher could be attached to the underside of the fore-end when required. The butt, handguard and pistol grip were made of fibreglass-reinforced nylon, and – profiting from US Army experiences in Vietnam – the bore and gas-tube were chromium plated to reduce the effects of fouling. Bipods and a folding skeletal butt could be supplied on request.

SR88A Introduced in 1990, this embodies several improvements suggested by field trials. The selector has three positions instead of four, the barrel is held in the receiver by a locknut and detent assembly, and the upper part of the receiver is pressed steel instead of forged aluminium.

SR88A Carbine Introduced to accompany the rifle, made only with a folding butt, this has a barrel measuring just 292mm (11.5in).

Assault rifle
Made by Chartered Firearms Industries, Singapore

Specification SR88
  Data from Ian Hogg, *The Greenhill Military Small Arms Data Book* (1999)
Calibre 5.56mm (.223in)
Cartridge 5.56x45, rimless
Operation Gas operated, selective fire
Locking system Rotating bolt
Length 970mm (38.19in)
Weight 3.66kg (8.06lb*) without magazine
Barrel 459mm (18.07in), 6 grooves, right-hand twist
Magazine 20- or 30-round detachable box
Rate of fire 750rds/min
Muzzle velocity 970m/sec (3182ft/sec) with standard ball ammunition

The 5.56mm R4 was based on the Israeli Galil, with changes made to suit local conditions.

The South African government obtained 7.62mm FAL-type rifles from Fabrique Nationale immediately after gaining independence from Britain in 1960. The earliest guns had plain muzzles without flash suppressors, and accepted a tube-hilt bayonet. In 1963, however, under the terms of a licence granted by FN to the South African Armament Corporation Pty (Armscor), the first indigenous rifles were delivered to the Defence Force from Lyttleton Engineering Co. Pty, of Pretoria. Known as the R1, these had a tube-frame butt folding to the right. The 1974-vintage R2 was simply a shortened form of the original rifle. Guns of this general type have been supplied to Lesotho; Rhodesia (Zimbabwe); South West Africa (Namibia) and Swaziland.

After protracted trials, the South African government adopted the 5.56mm Rifle 4 (R4) in 1982, to replace the 7.62mm R1. The new gun was a minor adaptation of the Israeli Galil (q.v.). The fore-end and pistol grip were made of fibreglass-reinforced plastic; the butt, steel on the original IMI guns, was similarly synthetic to reduce the effects of the hot South African climate. The butt was lengthened, and changes were made in the bipod, gas system, receiver and rifling to suit SADF requirements.

R5 Adopted in 1987 by the marines and the air force, and then taken by the army to supplement and eventually replace the R4, this 5.56mm rifle is similar to its predecessor excepting for the omission of the bipod and a 13cm reduction in barrel length. A typical R5 is about 875mm long and weighs about 3.9kg.

An R4 rifle in service with South African soldiers in scrubland bordering the Namib desert.

R6 This 1991-vintage adaptation of the R5, intended for issue to paratroops, tank and armoured-vehicle crews, is basically an R5 with the barrel shortened to a point where the rear of the flash-hider all but touches the front-sight/gas-port housing block. Overall length is merely 805mm.

Assault rifle
Made by Lyttleton Engineering Co. Pty, Pretoria

Specification Standard infantry rifle
  Data from John Walter, *Kalashnikov* (Greenhill Books 1998)

Calibre 5.56mm (.223in)
Cartridge 5.56x45, rimless
Operation Gas operated, selective fire
Locking system Rotating bolt
Length 1005mm (39.57in*) with butt extended
Weight 4.3kg (9.48lb*) with bipod, but without magazine
Barrel 460mm (18.11in*), 6 grooves, right-hand twist
Magazine 35-round detachable box
Rate of fire 675±75rds/min
Muzzle velocity 980m/sec (3215ft/sec) with US M193 ball ammunition

The R5 is a short-barrelled version of the R4. This particular gun lacks its magazine.

CETME, 7.62mm   Spain

The essence of this roller-delayed breech may be traced back to the German MG 42, and to experiments preceding the introduction of the MP 43 – the first modern-style assault rifle. 7.62x51mm CETME *Modelo* A rifles were made in Spain in the mid-1950s. They were essentially similar to the pre-production examples, firing automatically from an open bolt, but had a rotating carrying handle on the bolt tubes, and oblique-cut magazine housings. A licence was granted to NWM in the Netherlands in 1956, to take part in contemporaneous army trials that eventually resolved in favour of the FAL, and the Germans had also become very interested.

Modelo B The Spanish government adopted this version for service in 1958. A grenade launcher and a sheet-metal fore-end had been added, and the mechanism was simplified by firing at all times from a closed-bolt position.

Modelo C This was approved in 1965, after a decision to standardise the NATO cartridge instead of the lower-powered Spanish pattern had been taken. The rifle was strengthened to withstand additional chamber pressure and recoil impulse, and a combination flash-hider/grenade launcher was fitted to the muzzle.

In 1984, 7.62mm CETME rifles were superseded in Spanish service rifle by the 5.56mm *Modelo* L rifle, though re-equipment has been so gradual that large numbers of 7.62mm guns remain in the inventory of ancillary forces or are being maintained in store. Chad, the Congolese Republic, the Dominican Republic, Guatemala and Mauritania have all purchased substantial CETME-type rifles (principally *Modelo* C) for front-line service, whereas several Scandinavian countries, Pakistan and Portugal have acquired sizeable numbers for trials.

***Modelo* C Sniper** A few heavy-barrelled rifles have been fitted with optical sights and restricted to semi-automatic fire, but with no great success; the Mauser-type Santa Barbara C-75 rifle has been preferred by Spanish police and counter-terrorist units.

***Modelo* D** Introduced in 1978, this improved version of the C pattern served only as a development prototype for the *Modelo* E.

***Modelo* E** Developed in 1981–2, this was little more than a *Modelo* C with improvements to the ejector, sights and handguard. Greater use was made of synthetic parts and some guns had burst-firing capabilities. However, no series production was ever undertaken owing to a rise of interest in 5.56mm weapons.

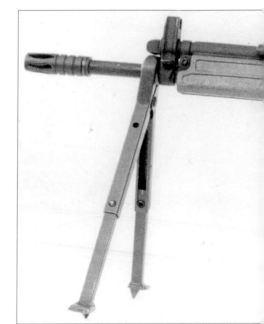

Modelo R A 1982-vintage short-barrelled 'port-firing' weapon, this was destined for the crews of tanks and armoured vehicles. The muzzle was adapted to fit a ball mount, the butt was replaced by synthetic cap, and the cocking handle was moved backward.

Assault rifle: Fusil d'Asalto CETME
Made in the Oviedo factory of Empresa Nacional de Militares Santa Barbara

Specification CETME *Modelo* C, wood-furniture version
Data from manufacturer's literature, *Assault Rifle INI CETME model C*, dated 1967

Calibre 7.62mm (.300in)
Cartridge 7.62x51 CETME or NATO, rimless
Operation Delayed blowback, selective fire only

Locking system Rollers on the bolt
Length 1015mm (39.96in*)
Weight 4.5kg (9.92lb*) with bipod and metal handguard, but no magazine; empty magazine, 275g (9.7oz*)
Barrel 450mm* (17.72in), 4 grooves, right-hand twist
Magazine 5- or 20-round detachable box
Rate of fire 550–650rds/min
Muzzle velocity 820m/sec (2580ft/sec*) with SS77 ball ammunition

A typical 7.62mm CETME Modelo E rifle.

Developed in the late 1970s, the perfected *Modelo* L shared the basic delayed blowback roller-lock system of the 7.62mm CETME. However, production was greatly simplified; the pistol grip was moulded integrally with the butt, for example, and a synthetic handguard was used.

The earliest guns had rotating four-position drum sights (100–400m), and used special 20-round magazines. Their selectors had an additional 'R' position, giving a three-round burst, but this was subsequently reduced to the status of an optional extra. In 1984, the *Modelo* L was adopted by the Spanish Army to

supplement and ultimately replace the 7.62mm rifles, the first guns being delivered in 1987.

Modelo L1 This was a minor variant of the L pattern – accepting the NATO standard US M16-type 30-round magazine – but was destined more for export than Spanish service. L1-type

The 5.56mm CETME Modelo L rifle.

The 5.56mm CETME rifles have proved popular with the Spanish Army and Special Forces.

rifles have three-position selectors and a simplified two-position backsight; bipods and optical sights have been used, but are not in general service.

Modelo LC A compact version of the basic assault rifle, with a 12.6in barrel with a short expansion chamber behind the flash suppressor. It also had a retractable butt. It was 33.85in long (26.2in with butt retracted) and weighed 7.05lb.

Assault rifle: Fusil d'Asalto Model L
Made in the Oviedo factory of Empresa Nacional de Militares Santa Barbara

Specification Standard *Modelo* LI
   Data from Ian Hogg, *The Greenhill Military Small Arms Data Book* (1999)
Calibre 5.56mm (.223in)
Cartridge 5.56x45, rimless
Operation Gas operated, selective fire

Locking system Rollers on the bolt
Length 927mm* (36.5in)
Weight 3.42kg* (7.55lb) with empty magazine
Barrel 400mm* (15.75in), 6 grooves, right-hand twist
Magazine 30-round detachable box
Rate of fire 750±50rds/min
Muzzle velocity 969m/sec* (3180ft/sec) with standard NATO ball ammunition

AG.42   Sweden

A typical AG.42B (Ljungmann) rifle.

This gas-operated rifle owed its adoption to the enlargement of the Swedish armed forces during the Second World War. A prototype Ljungmann rifle – said to have been based on Soviet Tokarevs captured in Finland – was given to an experienced production engineer, Erik Eklund, and work progressed so rapidly that the first AG.42 were delivered from the privately owned Husqvarna factory in 1942. This boosted Swedish rifle production without interrupting the flow of m/38 Mauser rifles from the government's Eskilstuna plant.

The AG.42 bolt, resting in a carrier, was cammed upward as propellant gas forced the carrier backward. Unlike most other pre-1945 rifles, gas had been taken from the bore to impinge directly on the bolt-carrier face – a system that was simple, but had a tendency to foul excessively. Thus the rifle never became

universal issue in the Swedish Army.

The Ljungmann rifle had a conventional full-length stock, with a handguard above the fore-end, as well as an unusual charging action: the sliding breech cover was pushed forward to connect with the bolt mechanism, then retracted to open the breech. The cover disengaged automatically at the end of its rearward stroke.

AG.42B Adopted in 1953, this had a stronger extractor, a refined trigger mechanism, a stainless-steel gas tube to reduce fouling, and a rubber roller on the right side of the breech cover to prevent damage to the cartridge cases during ejection. Minor changes were also made to the sights and magazine, but work ceased in the mid-1950s and the machinery was sold to Egypt (*see* Hakim).

Semi-automatic rifle:
Halvautomatiskgevar 42
Made by Husqvarna Våpenfabriks AB,
Huskvarna

Specification AG.42B
   Data from Ian Hogg and John Weeks,
   *Military Small Arms of the Twentieth
   Century* (seventh edition, 2000)
Calibre 6.5mm (.256in)
Cartridge 6.5x55, rimless
Operation Gas operated, semi-
   automatic fire only
Locking system Tilting bolt
Length 1215mm (47.80in)
Weight 4.74kg (10.38lb*) with empty
   magazine
Barrel 623mm (24.50in), 6 grooves,
   right-hand twist
Magazine 10-round detachable box
Rate of fire NA
Muzzle velocity about 745m/sec
   (2450ft/sec) with standard ball
   ammunition

Ak-5 (FN FNC)   Sweden

The 7.62mm *Automatkarabin 4* (Ak-4), a variant of the Heckler & Koch G3, was adopted in 1963, licences being acquired to permit production by Husqvarna Våpenfabrik and the government-owned Carl Gustafs Stads Gevärsfactori in Eskilstuna. The first Swedish-made rifles were delivered in 1965.

A reorganisation of the state-owned arms factories in 1971 created Forenade Fabriksverken (FFV or FFV Ordnance), allowing production of Ak-4 rifles to be concentrated in Eskilstuna. However, after trials spread over three years, the Ak-4 was superseded in 1984 by the Ak-5 – a minor modification of the FN Herstal 5.56mm FNC. The first deliveries of the new rifle were made in 1986, allowing the oldest of the Heckler & Koch patterns to be withdrawn.

Detail changes included enlargement of the trigger guard and cocking handle – facilitating use with arctic mittens – and the fore-end gained distinctive cross-hatching. The three-round burst-firing mechanism was sensibly discarded, and the metal parts were given a green enamel protective finish.

Assault rifle: Automatkarbin 5, Ak-5 Made by FN Herstal SA (1984–6), and Forenade Fabriksverken AS, Eskilstuna (1986 to date)

Specification Standard infantry pattern
Data from Ian Hogg and John Weeks, *Military Small Arms of the Twentieth Century* (Krause Publications, seventh edition, 2000)
Calibre 5.56mm (.223in)
Cartridge 5.56x45, rimless

Operation Gas operated, selective fire
Locking system Rotating bolt
Length 1005mm (39.57in) with butt extended
Weight 3.90kg (8.63lb*) without magazine
Barrel 450mm (17.72in), 6 grooves, right-hand twist
Magazine 30-round detachable box
Rate of fire about 650rds/min
Muzzle velocity 930m/sec (3050ft/sec) with SS109 ball ammunition

The Ak-5 is a modification of the FN FNC.

SIG SG 510 Switzerland

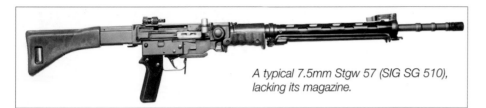

A typical 7.5mm Stgw 57 (SIG SG 510), lacking its magazine.

SIG has made a variety of auto-loading rifles, including the AK-53 – in which the barrel, once unlocked, was blown forward away from the standing breech. The first step to perfection, however, was made when the AM-55 was developed in the mid-1950s under the supervision of Rudolf Amsler. Inspiration for this rifle came from wartime German designs, specifically the StG 45 (M).

As the gun fired, the cartridge case thrust the bolt head backward until its two short rollers – originally round-tip flaps – were forced back into their housings against resistance offered partly by the angled entry of the flaps into the receiver wall and partly by the inertia of the heavy bolt body. Extraction was violent enough to demand a fluted chamber, but the weapon soon attained a reputation for reliability.

The prototype AM-55 rifle (subsequently renamed *Selbstladegewehr* [SG] 510-0)

was approved for service as the *Sturmgewehr* 57 or *Fusil d'Assaut* Mle 57. It was readily identified by straight-line construction, and a short ribbed plastic handguard beneath the barrel jacket. The sights could be folded.

Unfortunately, the rifle was expensive to make. Though it was heavy enough to mask the effects of the rapid breech stroke, and accuracy was very good, it fired automatically from a closed bolt and barrel heat had to be monitored to prevent 'cook off' ignitions. Work ceased in 1983 after about 585,000 had been made.

SG 510-1 An Stgw 57 chambering the 7.62x51mm NATO cartridge, this appeared in 1958 in the hope of attracting export sales. However, rigidly enforced Swiss neutrality posed problems and only a few were ever made.

SG 510-2 This was a lightened variant of the SG 510-1 with a wooden butt and a

slimmer barrel jacket.

SG 510-3 Chambered for the Soviet 7.62x39mm M43 round, but otherwise identical with its companions, this had a short barrel and a distinctively curved magazine. The bayonet stud lay on the barrel jacket behind the sight assembly. Changes to the woodwork and sights (eliminating the original straight-line configuration) were made shortly after the introduction of the SG 510-4 in the 1960s.

SG 510-4 Introduced in 1963–4, this chambered 7.62x51mm NATO ammunition. The wooden fore-end/handguard assembly, with a curved comb to the butt, sacrificed the advantages of straight-line layout to allow sturdier fixed sights to be fitted. The SG 510-4 sold well in South America, especially in Chile, but was too expensive to attract major purchasers.

SG 530 An unsuccessful 5.56mm derivative of the 510 series, introduced in 1967, this had a gas-piston assembly above the barrel to operate what had become a positive lock. Trials undertaken in 1971 showed that the breech mechanism was not suited to the high-pressure 5.56mm round, and that extraction problems would be difficult to overcome. A simpler gun with a rotating bolt was substituted.

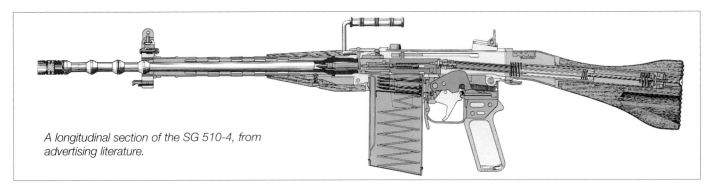

A longitudinal section of the SG 510-4, from advertising literature.

Assault rifle: also known as SG 510 or
Stgw 57
Made by SIG, Neuhausen am Rheinfalls

Specification SG 510-4
   Data from manufacturer's literature,
   SG 510 SIG, undated (*c.* 1972)
Calibre 7.62mm (.30in)
Cartridge 7.62x51 NATO, rimless
Operation Delayed blowback, selective fire
Locking system Rollers on the bolt head
Length 1015mm (39.96in*)
Weight 4.45kg (9.81lb*) with handguard
   and bipod; empty magazine, 300g
   (10.6oz*)
Barrel 505mm (19.88in*), 4 grooves,
   right-hand twist
Magazine 20-round detachable box
Rate of fire 500–650rds/min
Muzzle velocity 790m/sec (2592ft/sec*)
   with ball ammunition

The SIG SG 510-4 was essentially similar to the Stgw 57, though the similarity was hidden by cosmetic changes to the stock and fore-end.

The 5.56mm SG 530, retaining the roller-locking action, was not as successful as SIG had hoped.

SIG SG 540   Switzerland

Introduced in 1972, this replaced the unsuccessful SG 530. Limited quantities were made in the Neuhausen factory, but a manufacturing licence was sold to Manurhin in 1975, and the first French-made guns emanated from the Mulhouse factory in 1977–8.

The roller-lock system has been abandoned in favour of a rotating bolt.

The gas regulator is adjustable and a selector lever lies on the left side of the receiver above the pistol grip; markings can be seen through a small circular aperture. An optional three-round burst capability can be fitted, a Heckler & Koch-type drum backsight is used, a bipod folds under the fore-end, and special attention has been paid to

dismantling. Prototype rifles generally had wooden butts and handguards, but synthetic versions were soon substituted.

SG 540 The standard 5.56mm rifle could be obtained in fixed or folding-butt patterns. It was 950mm (fixed or extended butt) or 720mm (folded butt) long, and weighed about 3.3kg without magazine or bipod.

SG 541 Dating from 1979, this modified SG 540 was developed for trials against a rival Eidgenössische Waffenfabrik prototype. Made in two barrel lengths, the rifle had a synthetic skeleton butt, an integral bipod and a modified selector with the reference marks stamped conventionally into the outside of the receiver. The Swiss Army provisionally adopted the SG 541 in 1983, to replace the ageing Stgw 57, but lack of funding delayed progress and the work has subsequently concentrated on the SG 550.

SG 542 The standard 7.62mm version, described in the data panel.

SG 543 The short-barrelled derivative of the 5.56mm SG 540 lacked a bipod, measured 805mm (butt extended) or 570mm (butt folded) overall, and had a 300mm barrel.

The SG 530 was replaced by the 540 series, locked by a rotating bolt. This picture shows (left to right) *the 7.62mm SG 542, the 5.56mm SG 540 and the 5.56mm SG 543.*

Assault rifle
Made by SIG, Neuhausen am Rheinfalls

Specification Standard SG 542
Data from the manufacturer's
handbook, *Automatic Rifle SG 542
calibre 7,62x51mm NATO. Manual for
Instruction, Handling and Functioning
of the SIG Light Automatic Rifle,*
undated (*c.* 1980)

Calibre 7.62mm (.300in)
Cartridge 7.62x51 NATO, rimless
Operation Gas operated, selective fire
Locking system Rotating bolt
Length 1002mm (39.45in*) with grenade
launcher and flash suppressor
Weight 3.76kg (8.29lb*) with bipod, but
without magazine; loaded 30-round
magazine, 730g (1.61lb*); bayonet,
270g (9.5oz*); optical sight, 575g (1.27lb*)

Barrel 465mm (18.31in*) without flash
suppressor, 4 grooves, right-hand twist
Magazine 20-round detachable box
Rate of fire 650–800rds/min
Muzzle velocity 820m/sec (2690ft/sec*)
with SS77 ball ammunition

*The 540-series rifles were remarkable
for the ease with which they could be
stripped for cleaning.*

The two versions of the 550-series rifles used by the Swiss Army: the full-length StG 90 (SIG 550) and the shorter 'headquarters weapon' (SG 551).

Essentially an improved SG 541, these guns were adopted by the Swiss Army in 1984 as the *Sturmgewehr Modell 90.* The first series-made rifles were issued for service in 1986, replacing the ageing 7.5mm Stgw 57, and issue had been completed by 1996.

The SG 550 retains the operating system of the SG 540, but the previously optional three-round burst firing mechanism has been standardised. The plastic butt has a distinctive central void, a transparent plastic magazine is fitted, and a rail above the receiver accepts the customary Swiss optical or electro-optical sights. A NATO-pattern rail can be substituted if required. Bipods are also fitted as standard. A stud-and-slot system allows magazines to be clipped together, each being separated sufficiently far to enter the feedway individually.

SG 550 Sniper (SSG 550) The first of these rifles were made for evaluation in 1991. They have a heavy hammer-forged barrel, and a special adjustable trigger mechanism restricted to semi-automatic fire. The butt, cheek piece and pistol grip can be adjusted to suit the preferences of individual marksmen, and a variety of sights can be attached to the receiver rail. Most guns will be found with a 'mirage band', a detachable non-reflective strip above the fore-end which also minimises the disruptive effects of barrel heat on the sight picture.

The 5.56x45 SSG 550 is the sniper's version of the basic Swiss Army rifle. Note the heavyweight barrel, the cheek piece, and the palm-shelf on the pistol grip.

SG 551 This 'headquarters weapon' is basically a compact derivative of the infantry rifle, with the barrel cut to 357mm. It has also been advertised as the Stg 90 Assault Carbine, and a SWAT model, with a special optical/electro-optical sight rail, has been offered to police and counter-terrorist forces.

Assault rifle: SIG SG 550, Sturmgewehr 90 (Stg 90)
Made by SIG, Neuhausen am Rheinfalls

Specification Standard Stg 90 infantry rifle
   Data from Swiss Army handbook, *Das Sturmgewehr 90. Bedienungsanleitung, Wf. 50.222,* February 1984
Calibre 5.56mm (.223in)
Cartridge 5.56x45, rimless
Operation Gas operated, selective fire
Locking system Rotating bolt
Length 1000mm (39.37in*) with butt extended; 770mm (30.31in*) with butt folded
Weight 4.345kg (9.58lb*) with bipod and loaded 20-round magazine
Barrel 528mm (20.79in*), 6 grooves, right-hand twist
Magazine 20- or 30-round detachable box
Rate of fire 600–900rds/min
Muzzle velocity 980m/sec (3215ft/sec*) with US M193 ball ammunition

(Above) *The principle component group and accessories of the Swiss StG 90.*

(Left) *Issue of the StG 90 to the Swiss armed forces was completed in 1996.*

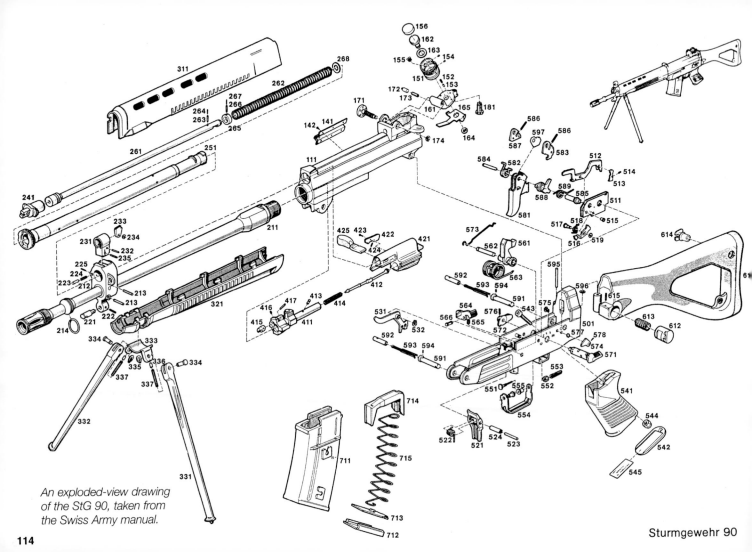

An exploded-view drawing of the StG 90, taken from the Swiss Army manual.

Sturmgewehr 90

SIG SSG 3000

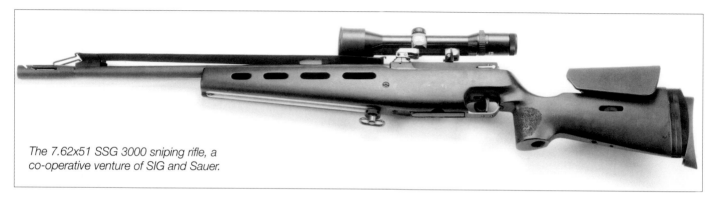

The 7.62x51 SSG 3000 sniping rifle, a co-operative venture of SIG and Sauer.

This rifle, introduced in 1992 to succeed the SSG 2000, was built around the Sauer 200 action, which reverted to a front-locking system. This was believed to offer better accuracy than the rear-locking 'wedge' lugs of the earlier gun.

Modular principles are used in constructing the SSG 3000, with a detachable barrel and a 'packaged' trigger mechanism. The wooden stock may be in a single piece or a warp-resisting laminate. The butt plate and cheek piece are adjustable, and four ventilation slots are cut laterally through the fore-end. A left-hand action may also be obtained, but is rarely seen in military service.

The trigger may be single- or two-stage type, the sliding safety catch locks the trigger, bolt and firing pin, and an indicator pin protrudes from the breech when a round has been chambered. The receiver rail is specifically designed to accept a 1.5-6x24 Hensoldt optical sight, but an alternative NATO-standard pattern can be obtained on request. SSG 3000 rifles can also accept mirage bands, bipods, hand-stops and sling anchors.

Bolt-action sniper rifle:
Scharfschützengewehr 3000, SSG 3000
Made by SIG, Neuhausen am Rheinfalls

Specification Standard infantry rifle
  Data from Ian Hogg and John Weeks,
  Military Small Arms of the Twentieth Century (seventh edition, 2000)
Calibre 7.62mm (.300in)
Cartridge 7.62x51 NATO, rimless
Operation Manual, single shots only
Locking system Rotating bolt
Length 1180mm (46.46in*)
Weight 5.4kg (11.88lb*) empty, without sights
Barrel 600mm (23.63in*), 4 grooves, right-hand twist
Magazine 5-round detachable box
Rate of fire NA
Muzzle velocity 800m/sec (2625ft/sec*) with commercial ammunition

Springfield M1903A3

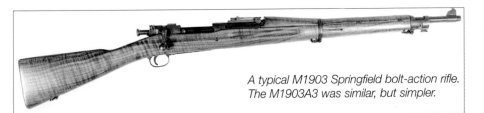

A typical M1903 Springfield bolt-action rifle. The M1903A3 was similar, but simpler.

This rifle was approved for service on 19 June 1903, though the backsight was changed in May 1905, a pointed 'spitzer' bullet appeared in October 1906 (changing the sight graduations), and a solid tubular backsight mount replaced the skeletal pattern in 1910. Work continued throughout the First World War, until the last rifle to be assembled in Rock Island Armory left the factory in June 1918. Military production at Springfield Armory had virtually ceased by 1927, though .30-calibre rifles were assembled for National Match target shooting and the NRA.

M1903A1 This was simply an M1903 fitted with a modified pistol-grip stock (Style C), which replaced the straight-wrist Style S with effect from 15 March 1929. The change in designation was authorised on 5 December, but few M1903A1 guns were made; straight-wrist stocks were still being used in 1939. A 'scant pistol grip'

was approved in 1942 to enable undersize or flawed stock blanks to be used.

M1903A3 Easily identified by a profusion of stamped and fabricated parts, this simplified M1903 was approved in May 1942. It had a straight-wrist stock without a grasping groove, and an aperture sight lay in an adjustable cradle on top of the receiver bridge behind the charger guides. The stamped trigger guard was deepened ahead of the trigger lever in 1943, but the production contracts were cancelled in February 1944.

M1903A4 Standardised on 14 January 1943, this sniper-rifle variant of the M1903A3 was made exclusively by the Remington Arms Company. The earliest examples had two-groove cut rifling, but later barrels used a four-groove draw-formed pattern. The bolt handle was bent downward to clear the 2.5x Telescope M73B1, made by the W.R. Weaver Company but carried in a Redfield

mount. The final batches of M1903A4 rifles were delivered in June 1944, owing to the approval of the M1C Garand.

Bolt-action infantry rifle; M1903A3
Made by the Remington Arms Co., Inc., Ilion, New York; L.C. Smith & Corona Typewriters, Inc., Pittsburgh, Pennsylvania; and the National Armory, Springfield, Massachusetts

Specification M1903
Data from the Ordnance Department *Description and Rules for the Management of the U.S. Magazine Rifle, Model of 1903, Caliber .30*, 1909 edition
Calibre 7.62mm (.300in)
Cartridge .30-06 (7.62x63), rimless
Operation Manual, single shots only
Locking system Rotating bolt
Length 1098mm* (43.212in)
Weight 3.94kg* (8.69lb), empty but including oiler and thong case
Barrel 604mm* (23.79in), 4 grooves, right-hand twist
Magazine 5-round internal box
Rate of fire NA
Muzzle velocity 823m/sec* (2700ft/sec) with M1906 ball ammunition

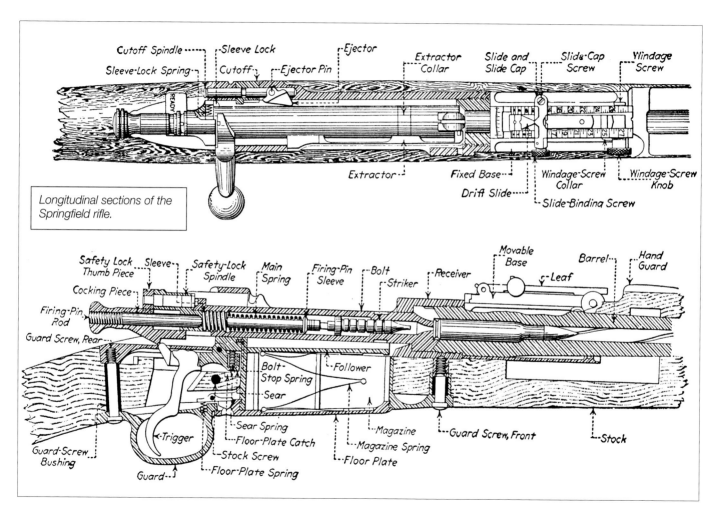

Longitudinal sections of the Springfield rifle.

Cutoff Spindle
Sleeve-Lock Spring
Sleeve Lock
Cutoff
Ejector Pin
Ejector
Extractor Collar
Slide and Slide Cap
Slide-Cap Screw
Windage Screw
Extractor
Fixed Base
Drift Slide
Windage-Screw Collar
Slide-Binding Screw
Windage-Screw Knob

Safety Lock Thumb Piece
Sleeve
Safety-Lock Spindle
Main Spring
Firing-Pin Sleeve
Bolt
Striker
Receiver
Movable Base
Leaf
Barrel
Hand Guard
Cocking Piece
Firing-Pin Rod
Guard Screw, Rear
Bolt-Stop Spring
Follower
Sear
Trigger
Sear Spring
Floor-Plate Catch
Stock Screw
Floor-Plate Spring
Magazine
Magazine Spring
Floor Plate
Guard Screw, Front
Stock
Guard-Screw Bushing
Guard

M1 Garand

Somewhere in northern France, a US soldier carrying a 2.36in rocket launcher and a Garand rifle watches for trouble.

The genesis of the Garand and its victory over the toggle-lock Pedersen rifle are related in the Introduction. However, though approved on 3 August 1933, the basic design was not perfected until trials of improved guns finished in October 1935. Only then was the M1 recommended for service, standardisation following on 9 January 1936. Teething troubles with individual parts delayed the first deliveries of machine-made guns until in September 1937 and a major redesign of the gas-cylinder assembly and barrel was authorised soon after sample rifles were badly received at the 1939 National Matches.

The M1 has a one-piece pistol-grip stock extending almost to the muzzle, with a handguard running forward from the receiver ring. The magazine lies within the stock, and a distinctive tangent-type backsight lies on top of the receiver behind the feedway.

Garand production by VJ-Day amounted to about 4.028 million; 600,000 or more were made immediately after the war, and work began again during the Korean conflict. A production licence was granted to Beretta (q.v.) in 1952 to make new guns to honour NATO/SEATO contracts.

Few changes were made in this period, though the M5 knife bayonet was approved in 1955. This had a small rearward-facing spigot on the upper part of the guard, which locked into the gas-plug housing beneath the barrel. Production finally ended on 17 May 1957.

M1C (M1E7) Standardised in July 1944, this sniper rifle had an M73 (Lyman Alaskan) or M73B1 (Weaver 330) telescope sight in a Griffin & Howe side mount. M1C rifles were often issued with the conical T37 flash-hider, subsequently standardised as the M2.

M1D (M1E8) This rifle, standardised for snipers in September 1944, was issued with the M81 or M82 optical sight – offering cross-hair and post graticles respectively.

M1E14 A shortage of M14 and M16 rifles in the early 1960s prompted the US Navy to develop a special chamber insert to enable the .30-06 M1 to fire 7.62x51 cartridges. A small sleeve was inserted in the front of the chamber to compensate for the shorter case-neck and different shoulder of the NATO round, being retained simply by firing two eight-round clips to expand it against the existing chamber walls. The first ten M1E14 rifles were successfully converted by the American Machine & Foundry Company in 1964.

Mark 2 Model 0 Dating from 1965, the production version of the M1E14 encountered insert-ejection problems. An improved insert was hastily developed by the Navy Weapons Production Engineering Center to cure the faults and work resumed; the American Machine & Foundry Company made more than 17,000 Model 0 guns before a modified Model 1 was adopted.

Mark 2 Model 1 This was an improved Model 0 with a better chamber insert. About 17,000 conversions were undertaken by the American Machine & Foundry Company and Harrington & Richardson.

Mark 2 Model 2 A designation applied to 8750 7.62x51mm Garand conversions with new barrels, supplied by Harrington & Richardson.

Semi-Automatic Rifle, Caliber .30, M1 Garand
Made by the National Armory, Springfield, Massachusetts; the Winchester-Western Division of Olin Industries, New Haven, Connecticut; Harrington & Richardson, Inc., Worcester, Massachusetts; and the International Harvester Corporation, Chicago, Illinois

Specification Standard M1
   Data from Ian Hogg and John Weeks, *Military Small Arms of the Twentieth Century* (seventh edition, 2000)
Calibre 7.62mm (.300in)
Cartridge .30-06 (7.62x63), rimless
Operation Gas operated, semi-automatic only
Locking system Rotating bolt
Length 1103mm (43.5in)
Weight 4.37kg (9.5lb) empty
Barrel 610mm (24.0in), 4 grooves, right-hand twist
Magazine 8-round internal clip-loaded box
Rate of fire NA
Muzzle velocity 853m/sec (2800ft/sec) with ball ammunition

A modern commercial M1 Sniper Garand, based on reconditioned wartime components.

An archive photograph of the prototype Winchester Light Rifle of 1940, showing how little it differed from the production version.

The M1 Carbine amalgamates a rotating-bolt action adapted from an experimental Jonathan Browning rifle submitted to the US Marine Corps with a short-stroke piston credited to David 'Marsh' Williams. Gas bleeds from the bore to strike a tappet, transferring energy to a spring-loaded operating slide. The slide rotates the bolt, which then runs back to eject the spent case and cock the hammer, then returns to strip a new cartridge into the chamber and rotate the locking lugs back into engagement.

On 30 September 1940, the experimental Winchester Carbine was recommended for immediate adoption; formal approval was forthcoming on 22 October and the gun was standardised as the Carbine, Caliber .30, M1. The initial requirement was set – most precisely – at 886,698 guns and, in November, contracts were placed with Winchester and the Inland Manufacturing Division of General Motors.

On 25 March 1942, Winchester licensed rights in the M1 Carbine to the US Government and, by 31 December 1943, with all nine facilities participating, nearly 3 million guns had been delivered; M1 Carbines were being made at a rate of more than 500,000 per month. As production was rapidly outstripping predictions, the projected Army Supply Program requirement was cut by a million guns and production at seven factories was terminated. After 1 June 1944, only Inland and Winchester continued to make carbines.

By the end of the war in Europe in May 1945, carbine production had exceeded 6 million. Many were eventually supplied to many foreign powers under the US Military Aid Programs, the most important recipients being South Korea and South Vietnam. Substantial numbers have also been used in Austria, Belgium, Taiwan, the Netherlands, Italy, France, Norway, Thailand, the Federal Republic of Germany, Uruguay, Greece, Burma and Indonesia.

The M1 Carbine has a pistol-grip half-stock with a handguard running from the receiver ring to the rear of the band. The box magazine protrudes ahead of the trigger-guard web, which contained a cross-bolt safety catch. The earliest guns had a two-position pivoting backsight and could not accept bayonets, but the approval of the Bayonet-Knife M4 (10 May 1944) required a new front band assembly incorporating a bayonet lug. This modification was soon made mandatory on guns returning for repair.

M1A2 The original rocking-L backsight, which provided two fixed range settings and had no provision for lateral adjustment, soon became the butt of criticism. Standardised in January 1943, the M1A2 (initially classified as M1E2) had an adjustable T21 backsight. However, as this required a modified receiver, adoption was rescinded in November and the sight was adapted to fit the standard M1.

M1A1 Experimental collapsible-stock carbines were developed in 1943 by Inland (known as M1E1) and Springfield Armory (M1E3 folding or M1E4 sliding). The M1E1 was subsequently made in quantity as the Carbine, Caliber .30, M1A1. It had a pistol grip and a skeletal butt with a reinforcing plate.

M2 An adaptation of the selective-fire T4, this was standardised on 23 October 1944, with a new 30-round box magazine and a selector on the left rear of the receiver. A T17 kit was subsequently developed to allow M1 Carbines to be converted in the field to M2 standards.

M3 Known during development in 1945 as T3, this was simply an M2 adapted for the infra-red Sniperscope M2. The earliest M3 Carbines had an infra-red lamp beneath the stock – ahead of the lamp-actuating trigger – instead of above it.

Owing to the end of hostilities and the cumbersome nature of the sight, production was small.

Semi-automatic carbine
Made by the Winchester Repeating Arms Company, New Haven, Connecticut; Inland Manufacturing Division of the General Motors Corporation, Dayton, Ohio; Rock-Ola Company, Chicago, Illinois; Quality

Private Billy Downs of the Headquarters Company, 89th Infantry Division, US First Army, anxiously seeks out German soldiers reportedly hiding in Werdau, April 1945.

Hardware & Machine Company, Chicago, Illinois; Irwin-Pedersen Arms Company, Grand Rapids, Michigan; Underwood-Elliott-Fisher Company, Hartford, Connecticut; Rochester Defense Corporation, Rochester, New York; Standard Products Company, Port Clinton, Ohio; International Business Machines Corporation, Poughkeepsie, New York; Saginaw Steering Gear Division of the General Motors Corporation, Saginaw and Grand Rapids, Michigan; and the National Postal Meter Company, Rochester, New York

Specification Standard M1 Carbine, post-1943
  Data from Department of the Army Technical Manual TM9-1276, *Cal. .30 Carbines M1, M1A1, M2, and M3*, 1953
Calibre 7.62mm (.30in)
Cartridge .30 M1 Carbine
Operation Gas operated, semi-automatic fire only
Locking system Rotating bolt
Length 904mm* (35.58in)
Weight 2.49kg* (5.5lb) with empty 15-round magazine; loaded 15-round magazine, 268g* (0.59lb)
Barrel 457mm* (18.0in), 4 grooves, right-hand twist
Magazine 15- or 30-round detachable box
Rate of fire NA
Muzzle velocity 579–610m/sec* (1900–2000ft/sec) with M1 Carbine ball ammunition

Suspended in 1951 by the intervention of the Korean War, work on a modernised Garand eventually created the T44 by amalgamating the action of the T20E2, the gas cylinder of the T25 and the magazine of the abortive T31. Tested extensively against the T25 and the FN FAL (T48 to the US Army), the T44 performed surprisingly well. Trials continued until, on 1 May 1957, the T44E4 was adopted as the 7.62mm Rifle M14 and the T44E5 was accepted as the heavy-barrelled M15.

The M14 is essentially similar to the Garand internally, though the detachable box magazine, shortened gas tube, and pistol-grip half-stock are most distinctive. The selector on many guns – unofficially known as M14 M(odified) – will have been plugged to restrict them to semi-automatic fire, though a standard three-position selector can be substituted when required. The earliest M14 rifles had wooden stocks and handguards, but the guard soon became ventilated fibreglass-reinforced plastic; finally, a durable synthetic stock was adopted and a ribbed non-ventilated handguard was used. Work ceased in 1963, and the production machinery was sold to the government of Taiwan in 1967.

M14A1 Introduced in 1960, this was a selective-fire M14 with a wood pistol grip behind the trigger, a bipod attached to the gas cylinder, a strap on the butt plate, and

The XM21 sniper rifle, photographed under trial in Rock Island Arsenal in January 1970, was a refinement of the M14.

The ready availability of parts allows Springfield Armory, Inc., and others to recreate M14-type rifle for competition use. This example approximates to the M21, but has a non-standard stock with an elevating comb and a bipod beneath the fore-end.

Semi-automatic rifle
Made by the National Armory, Springfield, Massachusetts; Harrington & Richardson, Inc., Worcester, Massachusetts; Winchester-Western Division, Olin Industries, New Haven, Connecticut; and Thompson-Ramo-Woolridge, Inc., Cleveland, Ohio

Specification Standard M14
  Data from Department of the Army Technical Manual TM 9-1005-223-12, *Operator and Organisational Maintenance Manual. 7.62-mm Rifle M14 and Rifle Bipod M2,* January 1963
Calibre 7.62mm (.300in)
Cartridge 7.62x51 NATO, rimless
Operation Gas operated, selective fire
Locking system Rotating bolt
Length 1125mm* (44.3in)
Weight 4.13kg* (9.1lb) with equipment and empty magazine; bipod, 794g* (1.75lb) extra
Barrel 559mm* (22.0in), 4 grooves, right-hand twist
Magazine 20-round detachable box
Rate of fire 750rds/min
Muzzle velocity 853m/sec* (2800ft/sec) with M59 ball ammunition

(on guns intended for use in support roles) a folding forward hand grip. The standard M14 action was used, but a stabiliser fitted over the compensator prevented use of the bayonet.

M15 Similar internally to the M14, the M15 had a heavy barrel, a fixed-leg bipod attached to the gas cylinder, a strengthened stock, and a folding shoulder strap on the butt plate. Made only in small numbers and comparatively unsuccessful in a light support role, the M15 was declared obsolete on 17 December 1959.

M21 Known during development as the XM21, this sniper-rifle derivative of the M14 was thoroughly tested against the Marine Corps Remington 700, the MAS FR-F1 and the Steyr SSG 69. The modified Garand proved to be as accurate as any of its rivals at long range, particularly when fired with M118 match ammunition, and so conversion of National Match (NM) pattern M14 rifles to XM21 standards began in Rock Island Arsenal in 1970. The XM21 was formally standardised in December 1975 as the M21, remaining the standard US Army sniper rifle until approval of the bolt-action 7.62mm Remington Model 24 in 1987.

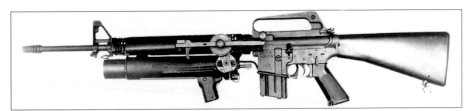

A full-length 5.56mm M16 rifle fitted with the abortive Colt CGL 40mm grenade launcher.

On 4 November 1963, Colt received the first large government contract for ArmaLite rifles – 85,000 XM16E1 rifles for the army and 19,000 M16 for the air force, the first batches being delivered in the spring of 1964.

They were similar to the preceding AR-15, excepting that the butt and handguard were blacked, the charging handle was changed to a T-bar, the firing pin was altered to minimise slam-firing tendencies, the flash suppressor was strengthened, and magazine bodies became alloy instead of steel.

Combat experience in Vietnam soon revealed problems. Though many were traced to lack of maintenance, persistent extraction failures and misfires due to the bolt carrier rebounding from the breech face were much more serious. The original buffer, composed of compressible ring springs, was replaced in December 1966 by a multi-weight pattern designed by Sturtevant. This alteration not only cured the rebound problem, but also reduced the excessive cyclic rate. Better propellant was adopted in May 1966, though fouling continued to plague the rifles until the original ammunition had been expended.

Colt was given a second contract, signed in June 1966 but later extended to 836,810 guns valued at $91.7 million; the future of the AR-15 was assured. The same company also supplied 40mm XM148 (Colt CGL-4) grenade launchers, but these were so unsuccessful that they had been replaced within two years by the AAI XM203 pattern. A new slotted compensator was approved in September 1966, and the XM16E1 was standardised as the M16A1 on 28 February 1967.

A chrome-plated chamber was approved to minimise extraction failures on 26 May 1967 and, on 30 June, the US government bought manufacturing rights from Colt. Reluctant to rely on Colt as the only supplier of ArmaLite rifles, the Department of Defense agreed provisional contracts with the Hydra-Matic Division of General Motors and Harrington & Richardson in April 1968. Other orders followed, despite unfounded worries expressed in Congress about the performance of Hydra-Matic in particular.

In addition to Canada, China, Korea, the Philippines, Singapore and Taiwan, all of which make guns of their own, ArmaLite-type rifles and carbines have seen service throughout the world from Australia to Zaire. Details may be obtained from Edward C. Ezell, *The Black Rifle* (Collector Grade Publications, second edition, 1994), or John Walter, *Rifles of the World* (Krause Publications, second edition, 1998).

M16A2 This arose from US Marine Corps requests for improvements in the basic infantry rifle. The Joint Services Small Arms Program acquired 50 Colt-made M16A1E1 rifles in November 1981, and the M16A2 was adopted in

November 1983. The backsight was changed, a heavy barrel was approved, the suppressor was redesigned to serve as a muzzle brake, the shape of the pistol grip was refined, and the stock was filled with nylon foam. A three-shot burst feature replaced fully automatic operation.

CAR-15 The original M16-type guns were offered commercially as the Colt Automatic Rifle, alternatively known as the Model 601. Later rifles, built on the M16A1-pattern action and known as AR-15A2 Sporter II (Model 711), were usually accompanied by five-round magazines.

CAR-15 HB M1 Also known as the Model 606, this heavy-barrel assault rifle weighed 7.5lb without its magazine or accessories. A Colt, modified BAR or standard M2 rifle-type bipod could be attached. The Model 606B was similar, but had a four-position selector and an additional burst facility. Several hundred were made for US Army SAWS trials.

CAR-15 Sub-machine Gun (XM177 series) Easily identified by a 254mm (10in) barrel, early examples of this gun may be found with a telescoping version of the conventional butt instead of the perfected tubular pattern. The US Army ordered a few thousand Commando guns (Colt Model 609) as early as 1966. The first examples had a long flash-hider with a small-diameter exit port, but the muzzle blast was unacceptable. Development of

a better muzzle attachment allowed the CAR-15 to be reclassified in January 1967 as XM177, or XM177E1 with the bolt-closing device. The perfected XM177E2 was an E1 with a 292mm (11.5in) barrel.

Though the XM177E2 was popular with the Special Forces, continual accuracy problems caused the project to be abandoned in 1970, though Colt subsequently offered fully automatic versions for police use. In the 1980s, however, renewed interest created an improved XM177E2 known as XM4.

A short-barrelled CAR-15 fitted with a British Davin Optics IRS 218 night sight.

M231 Port Firing Weapon
Standardised in 1979, this is easily distinguished by the absence of a butt – only the buffer protrudes from the rear of the receiver – and by a rapid-pitch screw thread on the front of the barrel casing that mates with a ball mount in the US Army M2 Bradley Fighting Vehicle. M231 guns can be dismounted in an emergency and fired by using the carrying handle as a rudimentary sight.

Assault rifle
Made by Colt's Patent Fire Arms Mfg. Co., Hartford, Connecticut; Harrington & Richardson, Worcester, Massachusetts; and the Hydra-Matic Division, General Motors Corporation, Ypsilanti, Michigan

Specification Standard M16A2
    Data from Ian Hogg, *The Greenhill Military Small Arms Data Book* (1999)
Calibre 5.56mm (.223in)
Cartridge 5.56x45, rimless
Operation Gas operated, selective fire
Locking system Rotating bolt
Length 1000mm (39.37in)
Weight 3.40kg (7.50lb*) without magazine
Barrel 508mm (20.0in), 6 grooves, right-hand twist
Magazine 20- or 30-round detachable box
Rate of fire 800rds/min
Muzzle velocity 948m/sec (3110ft/sec) with M193 ball ammunition

Ruger Mini-14

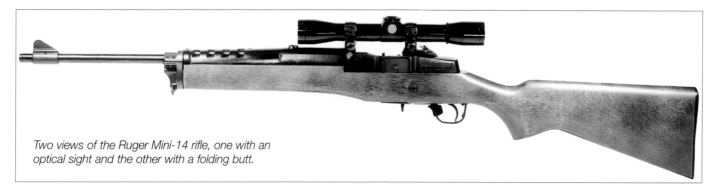

Two views of the Ruger Mini-14 rifle, one with an optical sight and the other with a folding butt.

Announced at the end of 1973, but not made in quantity until 1975, the militarised Mini-14 has a pistol-grip half-stock with steel liners to protect the mechanism; a safety catch through the front web of the trigger guard locks the hammer and sear.

Mini-14/5F A variant of the basic Mini-14 with a separate chequered-plastic pistol grip and a tubular metal butt, folding to the right.

Mini-14/5R The original Mini-14 had a conventional wooden handguard with the actuator sliding in an exposed channel on the right side of the fore-end. This was potentially dangerous, forcing Ruger to develop a fibreglass handguard/actuator cover in 1982. The Mini-14/5R also has a modified receiver with a folding-leaf backsight, patented integral optical-sight mount dovetails, and an improved buffer between the actuator slide and the receiver. The bolt stop has been modified to double as an ejector, eliminating the earlier spring-loaded ejector mechanism. The Mini-14/5RF, introduced in 1985, offers a separate pistol grip and tubular folding butt.

Mini-14/GB Dating from 1982, this was a semi-automatic variant with a flash-hider and a bayonet lug.

AC-556 Adapted from the Mini-14 in 1984, this gun incorporates a three-

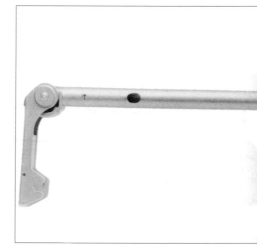

round burst-firing mechanism and an associated counter. The barrel is fitted with a compensator/flash suppressor, and a bayonet can be attached if required. The AC-556F has a tubular butt, folding to the right, and a short barrel with rifling making a turn in 254mm (10in). The magazine aperture of all AC-556 guns will accept standard M16-type 30-round magazines, as it has been configured in accordance with NATO standards. Stainless-steel construction was offered from 1986 onward, these particular options being given a K designation prefix.

Semi-automatic carbine
Made by Sturm, Ruger & Co., Inc., Southport, Connecticut, 1975 to date

Specification AC-556F
Data from Ian Hogg, *The Greenhill Military Small Arms Data Book* (1999)
Calibre 5.56mm (.223in)
Cartridge 5.56x45, rimless
Operation Gas operated, semi-automatic fire only
Locking system Rotating bolt
Length 815mm (32.08in), butt extended; 603mm (23.74in), butt folded

Weight 3.15kg (6.94lb*) without magazine
Barrel 330mm (13.0in), 6 grooves, right-hand twist
Magazine 5-, 20- or 30-round detachable box
Rate of fire 750rds/min
Muzzle velocity 1058m/sec (3470ft/sec) with commercial .223 Remington ammunition

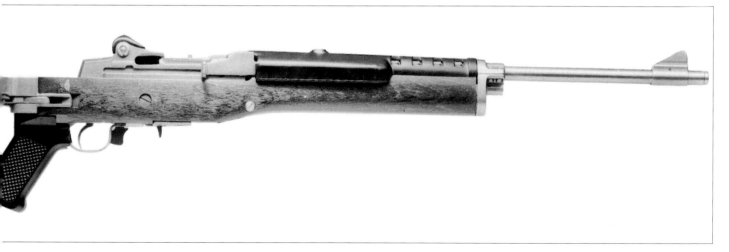

These guns were widely touted as the successors to the ArmaLites (q.v.), developed after Eugene Stoner and his development team had been lured away from the original promoters. The 7.62mm Model 62 of 1962 was a rotating-bolt auto-loader, with a gas piston replacing the original direct-impingement system.

The piston lay in a tube above the barrel, the charging slide and handle rode on rails on the left side of the receiver, and the furniture was wooden. Though optimistically advertised as part of a multi-weapon system, the Model 62 offered too little advancement over guns such as the FAL and orders were elusive. However, the rise of interest in small calibres and high velocity persuaded Cadillac Gage to develop a .223 Remington (5.56x45mm) version, entrusting work to James Sullivan and Robert Fremont.

Seen as an integral part of a weapons system, the resulting Model 63 rifle had great potential. It was heavier than the AR-15, but the long-stroke gas-piston system avoided most of the fouling problems of the ArmaLite while retaining adequate power to lift an ammunition belt in the machine-gun derivatives. The

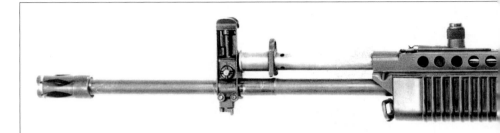

A typical 5.56mm Stoner Model 63 assault rifle, seen as part of a weapons system that ranged from a light carbine to a belt-fed machine-gun.

guns were all conventional, with charging handles on non-reciprocating slides. Wooden butts were fitted to the earliest guns, but later examples were synthetic.

The Stoner multi-weapon project was licensed in 1964 to Mauser-IWK AG, then transferred to NWM (a Mauser subsidiary) in 1965. However, flaws revealed in US Army trials forced improvements to be made in the Model 63.

Model 63A A 1968-vintage improvement of the original rifle, this had an ejection-port cover, an extended magazine housing, changes in the gas system, and a reciprocating charging handle on the receiver top that doubled as a bolt-closing device. The selector had only two positions, as a separate safety catch had been added.

Model 63A carbine Little more than a short-barrel version of the rifle, this had

a folding skeletal-tube butt.

XM22 A designation applied by the US Army to Model 63 rifles acquired for evaluation.

XM22E1 The perfected Model 63A Stoner rifle was tested extensively by the US authorities, but offered too few advantages over the established ArmaLite series to be recommended for adoption, though the XM207E1 light machine-gun was classified as limited standard.

Assault rifle
Made by the Cadillac Gage Corporation, 1963–9

Specification Standard Model 63
  Data from NWM advertising leaflet,
  Stoner 63A1 Assault Rifle, Cal.
  5,56mm, XM22 (undated, *c.* 1970)
Calibre 5.56mm (.223in)
Cartridge 5.56x45, rimless
Operation Gas operated, selective fire

Locking system Rotating bolt
Length 987mm (38.86in)
Weight 3.65kg (8.05lb) with empty
  magazine
Barrel 513mm (20.19in) excluding flash
  suppressor, 6 grooves, right-hand twist
Magazine 30-round detachable box
Rate of fire 800rds/min
Muzzle velocity 990m/sec (3248ft/sec*)
  with M193 ball ammunition

Remington M40A1 USA

The Remington M40A1 bolt-action sniping rifle, popular with the US Marine Corps.

This is a military adaptation of the standard Remington Model 700 sporting rifle, introduced in 1962 to replace the earlier 720 series developed in 1949–50 by a team led by Michael Walker. Adopted by the USMC in the mid-1960s, to replace M1C and M1D Garands, the M40A1 had a heavy barrel, a plain wood pistol-grip half-stock, and lacked iron sights. An optical sight was fitted to rails on the receiver-ring and bridge.

M24 Adopted in 1987 to replace the Garand-type M21, as part of the XM24 Sniping System, this improvement of the M40A1 has a Kevlar/graphite composite half-stock with an aluminium bedding-block in the fore-end; the butt plate is adjustable; and a rail for optical or electro-optical sights lies above the receiver. The M40X trigger mechanism is an adaptation of the M40 Match Rifle design, capable of adjustment, and the barrel is rifled specifically for the 173-grain 7.62mm M118 bullet. However, the M24 has been designed to be converted for .300 Winchester Magnum ammunition if long-term trials reveal better accuracy than the 7.62x51 NATO pattern.

Bolt-action sniper rifle
Made by The Remington Arms Company, Ilion, New York State

Specification Standard M40A1
  Data from Ian Hogg, *The Greenhill Military Small Arms Data Book* (1999)
Calibre 7.62mm (.300in)
Cartridge 7.62x51 NATO, rimless
Operation Manual, single shots only
Locking system Rotating bolt
Length 1117mm (43.98in)
Weight 6.57kg (14.5lb*) with sight
Barrel 610mm (24.0in), 4 grooves, right-hand twist
Magazine 5-round integral box
Rate of fire NA
Muzzle velocity 777m/sec (2550ft/sec) with commercial ball ammunition

The breech of a Mosin-Nagant 91/30 sniper rifle, showing the PU optical sight.

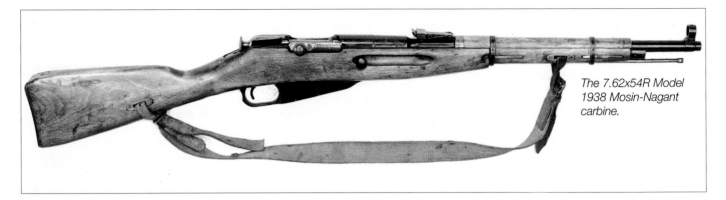

The 7.62x54R Model 1938 Mosin-Nagant carbine.

Revolution and civil war drove the arms industry perilously close to collapse. In July 1919, Trotsky warned that new rifles were in short supply, as White forces had captured Izhevsk; Sestroretsk had been evacuated, which left only the Tula facilities intact. The crisis had passed by September 1919, but a decision was then taken to standardise the 1891-pattern dragoon rifle once existing stocks of infantry rifle parts had been exhausted. The first new guns were to be made in Izhevsk in 1923, and in Tula in 1924.

Adopted on 28 April 1930, though trials had begun in 1924, the perfected 1891/30 Soviet version of the Tsarist dragoon rifle had a simplified cylindrical receiver and a hooded front sight. The one-piece straight-wrist stock retained the pre-1917 profile, but slotted oval sling anchors were

fitted in the butt and fore-end, and the barrel bands were held by springs instead of screws. The backsight was a new tangent-leaf design, and the socket bayonet, developed by Kabakov and Komaritskiy in 1928, had a spring catch instead of an archaic locking ring.

Finish on Soviet-made guns was notably poorer than on pre-1917 examples, but the obr. 1891/30g was solid and reliable. It was also more accurate at short ranges than its predecessors owing to greater care taken in calibrating the sights.

Partisan rifles A few Mosin-Nagants were used with 26mm-diameter rubber-baffle silencers weighing about 450g. These combinations could only fire subsonic 'partisan' ammunition, with green marks on the bullet, case or primer;

otherwise, baffles were wrecked after a few rounds.

Sniper rifle *(Snayperskaya vintovka)* The need for an efficient sniper rifle arose from attempts to develop marksmanship made during the First Five Year Plan. After 1932, therefore, guns selected for

accuracy had their bolt handles turned downward to clear the telescope sights and the side of the stock was appropriately cut away. The 4x PE sight had a 30mm objective lens and a field of view of 8 degrees; windage and elevation adjustments were internal. The earliest examples were mounted in a single-piece twin split-ring mount held on the receiver ring above the chamber, but this was replaced by a twin split-ring mount fitted to a dovetailed base-plate on the left of the receiver. Use of the PU telescope, introduced in 1940 for the Tokarev sniper rifle, was soon extended to the Mosin-Nagant. Shorter and lighter than the PE type, the 3.5x PU was carried in a twin-ring slab-side mount.

M1938 carbine Adopted in 1939, this replaced full-length rifles and surviving ex-Tsarist carbines in cavalry, artillery, signals and motor-transport units. It was basically a shortened infantry rifle and would accept the standard socket bayonet.

M1944 carbine Eight differing bayonets were tried on Mosin-Nagant carbines throughout May 1943. A preference for the Semin system, evident by November, allowed the obr. 1944g carbine to be standardised on 17 January 1944. It was identical with the preceding 1938 pattern, excepting for the special cruciform-blade bayonet pivoting on a block attached to the right side of the muzzle. Production soon ceased in the Soviet Union, but continued elsewhere – notably in China – until the late 1950s.

Bolt-action rifle: Vintovka obr. 1891/30g
Made by ordnance factories in Tula, Izhevsk, Sestroretsk and elsewhere

Specification Standard infantry pattern
Data from John Walter, *Rifles of the World* (second edition, 1998)
Calibre 7.62mm (.300in)
Cartridge 7.62x54, rimmed
Operation Manual, single shots only
Locking system Rotating bolt
Length 1231mm* (48.45in)
Weight 3.95kg* (8.71lb) empty
Barrel 730mm* (28.75in), 4 grooves, right-hand twist
Magazine 5-round integral charger-loaded box
Rate of fire NA
Muzzle velocity 805m/sec* (2640ft/sec) with standard Type D ball ammunition

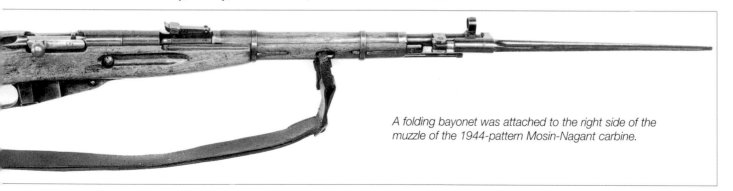

A folding bayonet was attached to the right side of the muzzle of the 1944-pattern Mosin-Nagant carbine.

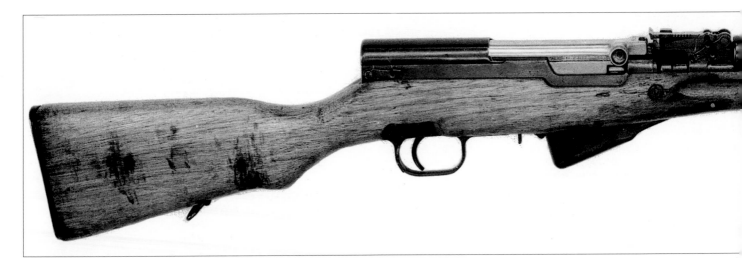

Mass production of the perfected SKS – a refined form of the original wartime version – did not begin until the spring of 1949, apparently as a safeguard against the failure of the Kalashnikov assault rifle. The SKS is a conventional weapon, with a pistol-gripped wooden stock (solid or laminated) and a distinctive folding bayonet beneath the muzzle. It is easily dismantled and has proved to be durable enough to withstand arduous service. The

magazine can be loaded with single rounds or from rifle chargers, guides for the latter being machined on the bolt carrier face; unloading merely requires the magazine housing to be unlatched and swung downward.

Sergey Simonov and his design bureau made many attempts to improve the SKS, but the success of the Kalashnikov assault rifle ensured that work had ceased by the mid-1950s. However, large numbers of SKS have

been made in Soviet-bloc countries, particularly in China and what was then Yugoslavia. Chinese Type 56 carbines usually have bayonets with long triangular-section blades, and some of the Yugoslav guns will display grenade launchers attached to the muzzle.

Semi-automatic carbine: Samozariadniya karabina sistemy Simonova (SKS)
Made by the state ordnance factories in Izhevsk and elsewhere

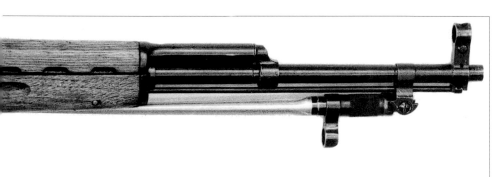

Specification Standard Soviet version
Data from the official Soviet Army
manual, *Nastavleniy po Strelkovomu
delu: 7.62mm samozariadniy karabin
simonova (SKS)*, Moscow, 1963

Calibre 7.62mm (.300in)
Cartridge 7.62x39 M43, rimless
Operation Gas operated, semi-
automatic fire only
Locking system Tilting bolt
Length 1020mm (40.16in*) with bayonet
folded; 1260mm (49.61in*) with
bayonet extended
Weight 3.75kg (8.27lb*) with empty
magazine
Barrel 520mm (20.47in*), 4 grooves,
right-hand twist
Magazine 10-round integral charger-
loaded box
Rate of fire NA
Muzzle velocity 735m/sec (2411ft/sec*)
with Type PS ball ammunition

*Two copies of the Soviet Simonov SKS: a Chinese
Type 56* (top)*, with its folding bayonet, and a
Yugoslav M59/66* (bottom) *with a grenade launcher.*

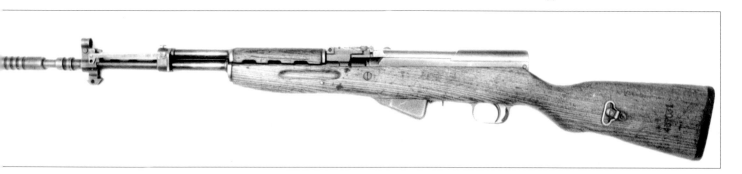

The 7.62x39 Kalashnikov has been made in many forms, including this Hungarian AMD-65.

The Kalashnikov has become one of the world's most popular weapons, serving not only regular forces with pro-Communist leanings but also countless terrorist groups from South America to the Far East. Production is said to have exceeded 50 million guns, and has been undertaken in many former Soviet-bloc countries. Modified guns have even emanated from Finland, Israel and South Africa.

The Kalashnikov action taps propellant gas at the mid-point of the bore to strike a piston attached to the bolt carrier. This drives the piston/bolt carrier assembly backward and rotates the bolt out of engagement. Widely criticised for its clumsiness, low muzzle velocity and a poor-performing cartridge (from the purely technical standpoint, validly), the Kalashnikov is simple, solid, reliable, and surprisingly effective when firing automatically.

The earliest guns incorporated extensive welding, stamping and pressed-metal parts, but an enforced change from stamped to machined components was made in 1951 as Soviet industry had been unable to master sheet-metal fabrication techniques gleaned from the Germans.

The rifles had wood butts and fore-ends, pistol grips originally being laminated wood (though often replaced with coarsely chequered or ribbed plastic varieties). Butt plates were steel, with a hinged trap, and a cleaning rod was carried beneath the barrel. Selectors were crudely marked with an electric pencil, and the

A Soviet AKS, made in Izhevsk in 1952, with its butt extended.

magazines, originally plain sided, were soon ribbed to increase body-strength.

A change was made to the rear of the receiver *c.* 1953, when, to strengthen the attachment, an extension was added to receive the tip of the butt. Laminated woodwork became standard. Selector markings were generally stamped, and shallow panels were milled in the sides of the receiver to save weight.

AKS This has a pressed-steel butt that folds down and forward under the receiver. It was particularly popular with airborne forces and tank troops.

Assault rifle: Avtomata Kalashnikova, AK
Made in the ordnance factories in Izhevsk, Tula and elsewhere, 1949–59

Specification AK, perfected version
  Data from John Walter, *Kalashnikov* (1999)
Calibre 7.62mm (.300in)
Cartridge 7.62x39 M43, rimless
Operation Gas operated, selective fire
Locking system Rotating bolt
Length 870mm (34.25in*)
Weight 4.3kg (9.48lb*) with empty magazine

Barrel 415mm (16.34in*), 4 grooves, right-hand twist
Magazine 30-round detachable box
Rate of fire 775±50rds/min
Muzzle velocity 710m/sec (2329ft/sec*) with M43 ball ammunition

Polish infantrymen with AK rifles take part in manoeuvres, 1971.

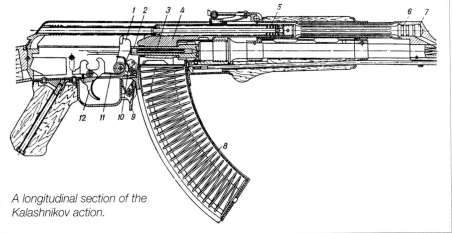

A longitudinal section of the Kalashnikov action.

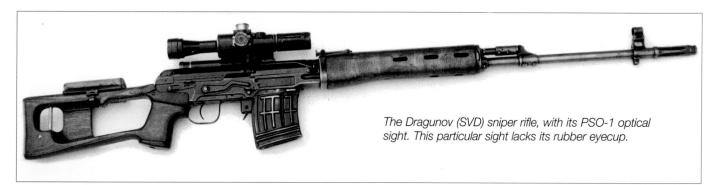

The Dragunov (SVD) sniper rifle, with its PSO-1 optical sight. This particular sight lacks its rubber eyecup.

Entering service in 1965, SVD rifles have been used wherever Soviet influence has been strong. Production has been undertaken in Bulgaria, the People's Republic of China, Egypt, Hungary and Poland; PSO-1 optical sights usually prove to have been made in the Soviet Union or the German Democratic Republic, but the Chinese may also make them.

Credited to a design team led by Evgeniy Dragunov and Ivan Samoylov, the Dragunov action relies on a rotating three-lug bolt adapted from the Kalashnikov and a short-stroke gas piston inspired by the pre-war Tokarev. The cutaway butt is combined with the pistol grip, the slender barrel has a three-slot compensator/muzzle brake, and the position of the gas port can be changed with a cartridge case rim. The trigger is a simplification of the AK type, lacking the ability to fire automatically. Ribs pressed into the sides of the box magazine improve the feed of the clumsy rimmed cartridges.

The 4x24 PSO-1 optical or 1-PN51 image-intensifier sights can be clamped on to a rail on the lower left side of the receiver, but the Dragunov is very light by modern sniper-rifle standards and its performance has been the subject of debate. However, rifles of this type are still seen as an integral part of infantry

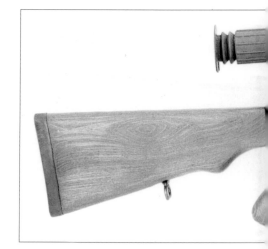

equipment – a tradition in the Soviet Army dating back to the early 1930s – and the SVD is capable of acceptable accuracy with good-quality ammunition.

Semi-automatic sniper rifle:
Snayperskaya Vintovka Dragunova, SVD
Made by the Izhevsk ordnance factory

Specification Standard Soviet pattern
Data from John Walter, *Kalashnikov* (1999)

Calibre 7.62mm (.300in)
Cartridge 7.62x54, rimmed
Operation Gas operated, semi-automatic fire only
Locking system Rotating bolt
Length 1220mm (48.03in*)
Weight 4.3kg (9.48lb*) with empty magazine and PSO-1 sight
Barrel 545mm (21.46in*), 4 grooves, right-hand twist
Magazine 10-round detachable box
Rate of fire NA

Muzzle velocity 830m/sec (2723ft/sec*) with standard Type L ammunition

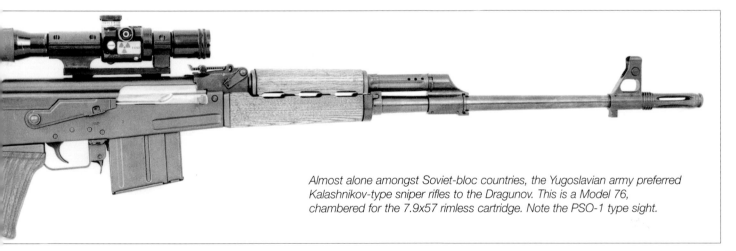

Almost alone amongst Soviet-bloc countries, the Yugoslavian army preferred Kalashnikov-type sniper rifles to the Dragunov. This is a Model 76, chambered for the 7.9x57 rimless cartridge. Note the PSO-1 type sight.

Once Soviet industry had mastered appropriate metalworking techniques, a modified Kalashnikov *Avtomat* was introduced in 1959. The stamped-steel receiver – a sturdy U-shaped pressing – was much lighter than the original machined forging, the bolt-lock recesses were riveted in place, and the stamped receiver cover was prominently ribbed. The gas-piston tube had semicircular vents immediately behind the gas-port assembly instead of the circular holes on the AK; and the bolt carrier was phosphated. The charging handle and pistol grip were made of plastic, though the butt and fore-end were usually laminated wood. Magazines were ribbed sheet-metal, then orange-red plastic.

The most important change was the incorporation of a rate-reducer in the trigger system, often mistakenly identified as an additional mechanical safety. By holding back the hammer after the bolt-carrier had depressed the safety sear, this reduced the rate of fire by about 15 per cent. But it also added unnecessary complexity to an essentially simple design.

A short oblique-cut compensator was added in the early 1960s to prevent the gun climbing to the right when firing automatically. At much the same time, the fore-end was broadened to improve grip, and a bracket was eventually added on the left side of the receiver to accept NSP-2 infra-red or NSPU image-intensifier sights. Some AKM have been fitted with single-shot GP-25 grenade launchers, under the fore-end, and have grenade-launching sights above the gas tube. A special butt pad minimises the effects of recoil.

AKMS Distinguished by a folding butt with three rivets and a long flute on each side of the strut, this replaced the AKS. The butt swings down and forward.

AKM, silenced Some guns will be encountered with the PBS-1 silencer and a special backsight leaf adapted to subsonic ammunition. The two-chamber silencer relied on a rubber plug and a series of baffle plates to reduce noise.

AKMS-U Made only in 1975–9, this compact short-barrel derivative of the AKM is merely 723mm (28.45in) long with the butt extended. The backsight is a simple rocking-L set for 100m and 500m; its base is combined with the receiver-cover pivot. A chequered plastic pistol grip accompanies a short wooden thumbhole fore-end, a

A typical Soviet AKM. Note that the construction appears to be much lighter than the AK, owing to the inclusion of so many stamped and pressed components.

short finned expansion chamber at the muzzle is fitted with a conical flash-hider, and the front-sight block (with a sling bar on the left side) has been moved back to abut the barrel guard. The AKMS-U can double as a port-firing weapon in some Soviet armoured personnel carriers.

Assault rifle: Avtomata Kalashnikova Modificatsionniya, AKM
Made by the Izhevsk ordnance factory, 1959–75

Specification Standard AKM
  Data from John Walter, *Kalashnikov* (1999)
Calibre 7.62mm (.300in)
Cartridge 7.62x39 M43, rimless
Operation Gas operated, selective fire

Locking system Rotating bolt
Length 878mm (34.57in*)
Weight 3.85kg (8.49lb*) without magazine
Barrel 415mm (16.34in*), 4 grooves, right-hand twist
Magazine 30-round detachable box
Rate of fire 620-680 rds/min
Muzzle velocity 710m/sec (2329ft/sec*) with M43 ball ammunition

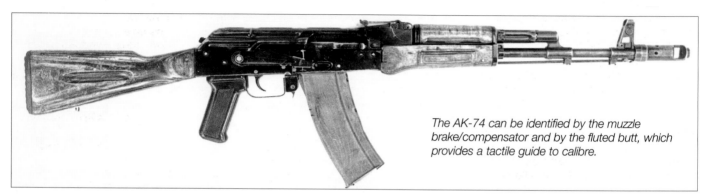

The AK-74 can be identified by the muzzle brake/compensator and by the fluted butt, which provides a tactile guide to calibre.

Experiments with 5.56mm M16 rifles captured in Vietnam in the 1960s convinced the Soviet authorities that the 7.62x39 M43 cartridge was ineffectual. By 1973, therefore, a 5.45mm version had appeared. Its two-piece bullet had a hollow tip within the jacket, to improve lethality by deforming against a target.

The AK-74 has an enlarged muzzle brake/compensator, which eventually gained two angled ports (with the larger of the two to the left to prevent the AK-74 climbing to the right when firing automatically). Flutes cut into both sides of the butt allow the calibre to be identified by touch, and lugs beneath

the barrel accept an improved wire-cutter/tool bayonet. A bracket for the 1-PN29 telescope sight can be attached to the left side of the receiver, or, alternatively, a single-shot GP-25 grenade launcher and an associated backsight could be fitted to the fore-end and gas tube.

The earliest guns retained butts and fore-ends made of wood laminate or resin-impregnated wood fibres, but these were soon replaced by synthetic furniture.

AK-74M (*Modernizovanniya, modernised*) This was developed in the late 1980s as a universal-issue replacement for the AK-74 and the

AKS-74. The butt retains the conventional shape, but can be swung forward along the left side of the receiver, rigidity in the extended position being enhanced by a special cam-locking catch mechanism. The AK-74M has distinctive plastic furniture, and a rail on the left side of the receiver to receive 1-PN29 optical, 1-PN51 passive infra-red or 1-PN58-2 intensifier sights.

AK-74N A standard AK-74 with a mount on the receiver for the 1-PN29 optical, NSP-2 infra-red, NSP-3 and 1-PN58-2 electro-optical sights.

AKS-74 Popular with parachutists and vehicle crews, this has a triangular skeletal butt that folds back along the left side of the receiver, reducing overall length to 700mm (27.55in).

AKS-74N This was simply a folding-butt version of the AK-74N, accepting the same variety of sights.

AKS-74U This short-barrelled gun superseded the AKMS-U in 1979. It measures merely 675mm (26.55in) overall and weighs only about 2.7kg (6lb) with an empty magazine. The rocking-L backsight and the pivoting breech cover/backsight base unit of the AKMS-U have been retained, but pressing a catch on the left side of the receiver behind the pistol grip allows an AKS-74 type skeletal butt to fold back along the receiver. The AKS-74U also has a short cylindrical barrel extension, apparently to act as an expansion chamber and reduce the violence of the muzzle blast.

AK-74UB Derived from the AK-74 in the late 1970s, this was adapted to fire a noiseless SP-3 'piston seal' cartridge.

AKS-74UN Dating from 1979, this was a variation of the AKS-74U fitted with a mount for optical or electro-optical sights. Owing to the shortness of its barrel, the AKS-74UN is best used at comparatively short ranges.

AKS-74Y A modified design with a semi-integral silencer attached to its shortened barrel, this gun has its fore-end and barrel casing cut back accordingly. A silenced bolt-action grenade launcher can be fitted beneath the fore-end, accompanied by a special grenade-launching adaptor on the backsight leaf.

AK 101 Though reports have suggested that the Kalashnikov is to be replaced in Russian service with the AN-94 (Nikonov) assault rifle when funds permit, the manufacture of more than 50 million AK, AKM and AK-74 weapons suggests that there is still life in a design of proven durability.

A variant of the AK-74M entered in the Russian Abakan trials has provided the basis for the Hundred-series Kalashnikovs announced in 1995. Chambered for the 5.56x45 round, in the hope of attracting export orders, the AK 101 has a new burst-firing capability, a refined muzzle brake/compensator unit, and minor improvements to the plastic furniture.

AK 102 This short-barrelled version of the 5.56mm AK 101, comparable with the Soviet AKM-SU, apparently has a short flash-hider and a simplified 300m (330yd) sight carried on an extension of the backsight block running back above the ejection port.

AK 103 Intended for export to agencies which retain the original 7.62x39 M43 cartridge, this full-length rifle is otherwise comparable with the AK 101. The curved magazine is an identifying feature.

AK 104 A short-barrelled version of the 7.62mm AK103.

AK 105 The only current representative of the Hundred-series Kalashnikovs to chamber the 5.45x39 cartridge, this is really little more than a short-barrelled version of the AK-74M.

Assault rifle: Avtomata Kalashnikova obr. 74, AK-74
Made by the state ordnance factories

Specification Standard AK-74
Data from John Walter, *Kalashnikov* (1999)
Calibre 5.45mm (0.215in)
Cartridge 5.45x39 M74, rimless
Operation Gas operated, selective fire
Locking system Rotating bolt
Length 956mm (37.64in*)
Weight 4.85kg (10.69lb*) with loaded
40-round magazine
Barrel 415mm (16.34in*), 4 grooves,
right-hand twist
Magazine 30- or 40-round detachable box
Rate of fire 620–680rds/min
Muzzle velocity 900m/sec (2953ft/sec*)
with B-74 ball ammunition

Glossary

Accelerator. A mechanism which increases the rearward velocity of the recoiling bolt to separate it more quickly from a recoiling barrel.

Auto-loading, self-loading or semi-automatic. A mechanism that unlocks the breech (if appropriate), extracts and ejects the empty case, then re-cocks the firing mechanism and re-loads.

Automatic rifle. A gun which will continue firing until either the trigger is released or the ammunition has been expended.

Blowback, or case projection. A system in which closure of the breech is undertaken simply by the inertia of the breech-block and pressure from the return spring.

Bolt. A means of closing the breech of a gun, this will be found on virtually all military rifles. Most bolts have a cylindrical body with lugs to rotate into the receiver.

Bolt action. A system of operation relying on a bolt reciprocating to extract, eject, reload and cock the firing mechanism.

Bore. The axial hole through the barrel, usually rifled to spin the projectile. Bore diameter measurements usually exclude the depth of the rifling.

Breech-block. Any non-cylindrical means of closing a breech.

Breech. The rear end of the action, containing the breech block and giving access to the chamber.

Butt. The part of the stock extending backward against the firer's shoulder. The upper edge of the butt is known as the comb.

Carbine. A firearm with a barrel measuring less than 20-22in.

Chamber. The shaped area of the interior of the gun barrel at the breech, into which the cartridge fits.

Charger. A loading device that holds cartridges in a sheet-metal strip from which they can be pressed downward into a magazine box. Misleadingly known as 'clip' in North America.

Clip. A loading device holding several cartridges, the entire assembly being placed in the magazine. Cf 'charger'.

Compensator. A muzzle fitting designed to divert emerging gas upward, counteracting the rise of the muzzle during rapid firing.

Cyclic rate, or rate of fire. The theoretical continuous rate of fire of an automatic weapon, assuming an unlimited supply of ammunition.

Delayed blowback. A modified blowback mechanism with an additional restraint or brake placed on the bolt or similar breech system to delay or slow the opening movement.

Disconnector. A component in the trigger mechanism which disconnects the trigger from the remainder of the firing train after each shot.

Ejector. A device to throw empty cases out of a gun. It is usually a fixed bar or blade which intercepts a spent case withdrawn from the breech by the extractor.

Extractor. Customarily a claw attached to the bolt or breech block, this engages the rim or groove to draw the cartridge case from the chamber.

Flash-hider or suppressor. A muzzle attachment designed to minimise the effects of propellant flash, generally by using prongs or a pierced tube.

Gas operation. A method of operating an auto-loader by tapping part of the propellant gas from the bore to unlock the breech and propel the bolt or breech-block backward.

Loaded-chamber indicator. A pin, blade or other device to give visual and tactile indication that there is a cartridge in the chamber.

Magazine. The container in which the cartridges are held to permit continuous fire. Military-rifle magazines may be loaded from chargers ('stripper clips') or with clips.

Muzzle brake. An attachment similar to a compensator, intended to turn the emerging gases and drive them rearward.

Operating cycle. The complete functioning routine of an automatic weapon.

Recoil. A force generated by firing, opposing the forward motion of the projectile.

Recoil operation. Recoil forces can be harnessed to operate an auto-loading action. Long recoil relies on the barrel and breech recoiling locked together for a distance at least as long as a complete unfired cartridge. At the end of this stroke, the bolt is unlocked and held while the barrel runs back to its forward position. Short recoil is similar to long recoil, but the distance traversed by the components before unlocking occurs is less than the length of a complete unfired cartridge.

Rifling. The means by which spin is imparted to a bullet prior to emerging from the muzzle. Rifling generally comprises grooves separated by lands.

Sear. An intermediate component linking the trigger with the hammer or firing pin, holding the latter back until released by trigger pressure.

Selective-fire. A gun that may, when required, fire single shots, multi-shot bursts or fully automatically.

Semi-automatic rifle. A gun that fires once for each pull on the trigger and reloads automatically, but requires the trigger lever to be released before the next shot.

Stock. The part of the gun that contains or supports the barrel and action. Originally wood, military stocks are now generally synthetic.

Striker, or firing pin. This is driven by a spring to acquire enough energy to ignite a cartridge primer.

Tang. A rearward extension of the receiver, usually anchoring the butt to the receiver or frame.